# AMAZING BOOK OF
# QUESTIONS & ANSWERS

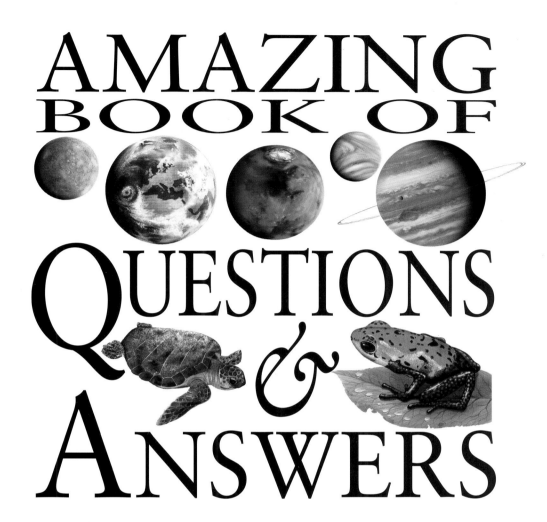

# AMAZING
## BOOK OF

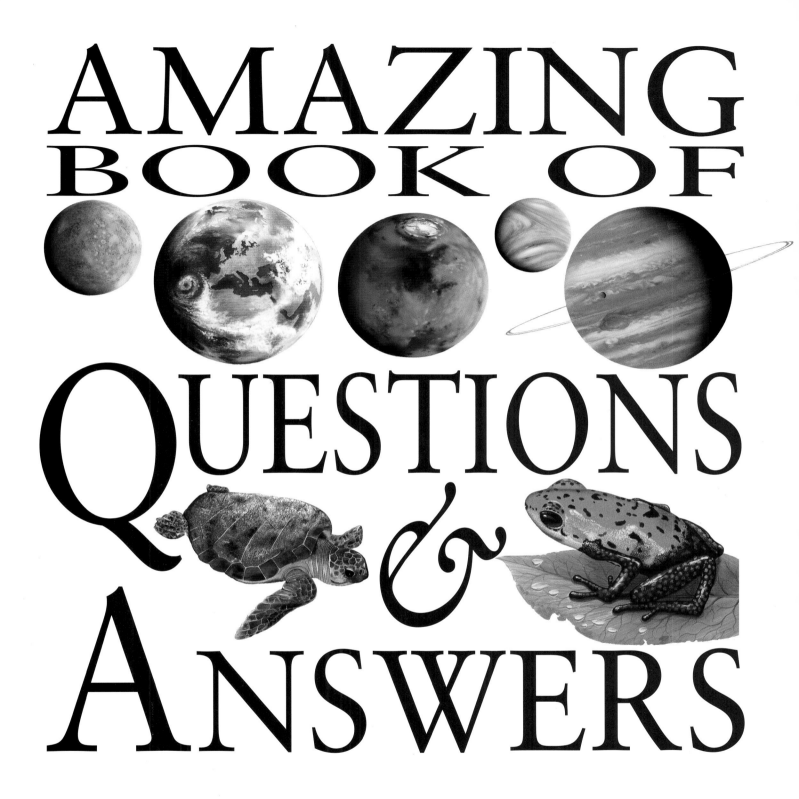

# QUESTIONS & ANSWERS

WHITECAP BOOKS

This edition published in Canada by
Whitecap Books Vancouver
351 Lynn Avenue
North Vancouver BC
Canada V7J 2C4
Phone (604) 980 9852  Fax (604) 980 8197

Whitecap Books Toronto
Phone (416) 444 3442  Fax (416) 444 6630

A Parragon Book, Parragon, Queen Street House, Bath BA1 1HE, UK

Copyright © Parragon 2000

Produced by Miles Kelly Publishing Ltd
Bardfield Centre, Great Bardfield, Essex CM7 4SL

Created, Written and Designed by
John Farndon and Angela Koo for Barnsbury Books

British Library Cataloguing-in-Publication Data

A catalogue record for this book is available from the British Library.

ISBN 1-55285-134-6

Printed in Indonesia

# CONTENTS

# AMAZING QUESTIONS

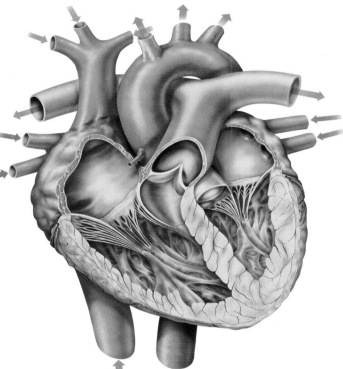

1. How many chambers has the heart?

## Why questions?

THE WORLD IS A WONDERFUL AND FASCINATING PLACE yet all too often we are told not what we want to know about – what makes us curious – but what someone wants to tell us about. In this book, we pose the kind of questions that you might

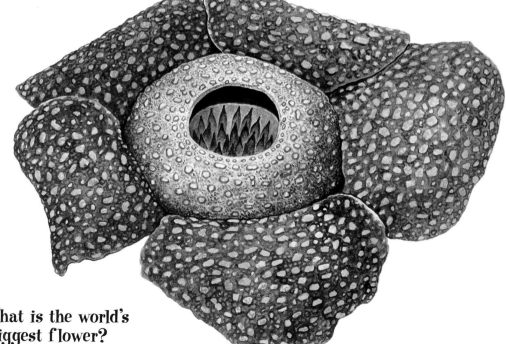

2. What is the world's biggest flower?

## 3. What's the smallest planet?

## 4. What's the Earth's core made of?

## 5. What's the smallest bit of an element?

ask if you had the chance – and answer these. On every spread too, there is a series of questions that we ask you – to give you a chance to test your general knowledge – or to challenge your friends and family. Here are some to get you going.

## 6. What is the world's biggest reptile?

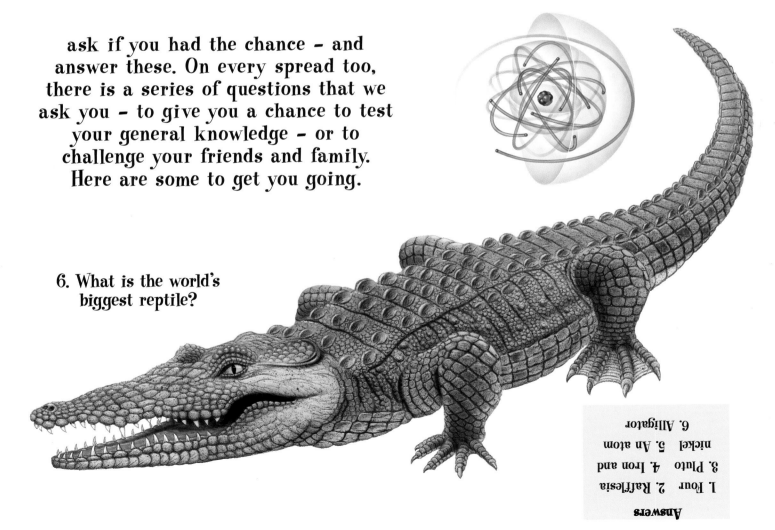

**Answers**

1. Four  2. Rafflesia  3. Pluto  4. Iron and nickel  5. An atom  6. Alligator

How did scabious
get its name?

There are
exploding
cucumbers in the
jungle: true or
false?

What tree is the
national symbol of
Canada?

Can plants cure
cancer?

What plant has two
different flowers?

Where does
chocolate come
from?

Which woodland
plant is good for a
kiss?

What plant amputates its own branches?

# Plants

What plants have their own water tanks?

What is the strongest rope in the jungle?

Why don't all trees lose their leaves?

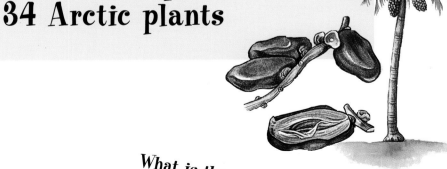

What is the world's biggest flower?

9

# Plants of all kinds

## What are plants?

THERE ARE MORE THAN 270,000 KINDS of plant around the world, ranging from tiny single-celled organisms to giant trees, the largest living things. Most have green leaves and can make their own food from sunlight, which is why most don't need to move around like animals. But some microscopic plants can move like animals, even though they can make their own food, while others cannot move, but steal food off other plants.

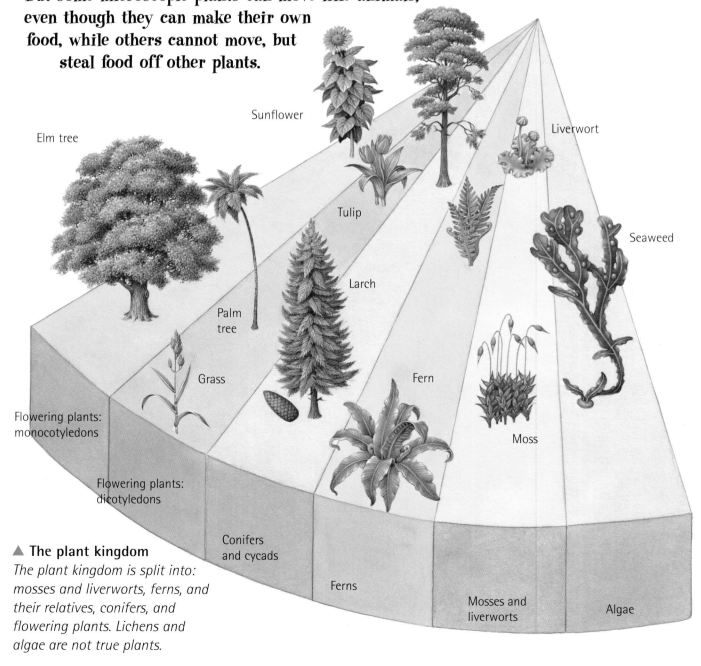

Sunflower

Liverwort

Elm tree

Tulip

Seaweed

Palm tree

Larch

Grass

Fern

Flowering plants: monocotyledons

Moss

Flowering plants: dicotyledons

Conifers and cycads

▲ **The plant kingdom**
*The plant kingdom is split into: mosses and liverworts, ferns, and their relatives, conifers, and flowering plants. Lichens and algae are not true plants.*

Ferns

Mosses and liverworts

Algae

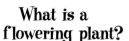

▶ **Flowering tree**
*Deciduous trees like this bottlebrush are among more than 240,000 species of flowering plant.*

## What is a flowering plant?

Flowering plants are plants that have flowers to make the seeds and fruits from which new plants will eventually grow. This doesn't only mean garden and wild flowers, but every herb, grass, fruit, shrub, and vegetable—all of which have tiny flowers. Another name for flowering plants is angiosperms.

## Are any big plants not flowering plants?

Yes. Plants that make their seeds in cones, rather than in flowers. These cone-bearing plants or conifers are also known as gymnosperms. They include trees such as pines.

## What are monocotyledons?

Flowering plants are either monocotyledons or dicotyledons. Monocotyledons begin from seeds with just a single leaf. They also tend to have longer, narrower leaves, like grasses, tulips, and daffodils. Dicotyledons start with two or more leaves from their seeds. Most flowering plants are dicotyledons.

## Do all plants grow from seeds?

No, only flowering plants and conifers do. Ferns and mosses grow from tiny cells called spores, which can be seen only under a microscope.

## Why are plants green?

Plants are green because they contain a green substance called chlorophyll. This plays a vital role in photosynthesis, the process by which plants make their food by absorbing sunlight. In photosynthesis, the plant changes carbon dioxide from the air, and hydrogen from water, into energy-giving sugars.

## What is the stem?

A plant's stem not only supports the flowers and leaves; it is also a pipe to take water, minerals, and food up and down between the leaves and the roots. Water goes up through tubes called xylem. Food goes down to the roots through tubes called phloem. In herbaceous plants, the stem is soft and green. In woody plants like trees it is stiff, and often covered in bark.

◀ **Conifer**
*Conifers like pines are among the oldest of all plants, appearing 275 million years ago.*

# QUIZ

1 What are the biggest plants?

2 Seaweeds are a kind of algae: true or false?

3 How do plants get water?

4 Some plants eat meat: true or false?

5 Plants that take their food from other plants are called a) felons b) parasites c) clingers?

6 Some ferns can grow as big as trees, more than 80 feet (25m) tall: true or false?

7 Plant spores can survive in outer space: true or false?

8 The oldest known plant is a creosote plant in California. It is thought to be: a) 250 years old, b) 1,260 years old c) 11,700 years old?

**Answers**
1. Trees 2. True 3. Through their roots 4. True 5. b)
6. True 7. True 8. c)

# Flowering plants

## What are flowering plants?

FLOWERING PLANTS are not just garden flowers and wild flowers with pretty blooms, but every herb, grass, shrub, tree, fruit, and vegetable too. Indeed, nearly every plant except ferns, mosses, lichens, and fungi is a flowering plant. The flowers may not be obvious but all have flowers that create the seeds and fruits from which new plants will grow.

▲ The largest seeds
*The largest seeds are double coconuts, weighing up to 40 pounds (18kg).*

### How do flowers make seeds?

Just as there are male and female animals, so a flower has male parts, known as stamens, and female parts, known as pistils. Seeds for new plants are made when pollen from the stamens meets eggs in the pistils.

### Where are a flower's sex organs?

The female parts or pistil, containing the ovaries where eggs are made, is the thick, short stalk in the middle of the flower. The male parts, or stamens, which make pollen, are the spindly stalks round it.

### Can flowers pollinate themselves?

Many flowers have both male and female parts. So some flowers can indeed pollinate themselves, and the pollen moves from the stamens to the pistil on the same plant. This is called self-pollination. Most flowers, however, are cross-pollinating. This means the pollen must be carried from the stamens of one plant to the pistil of another plant of the same kind.

### Why are flowers such pretty colors?

Pollen from some flowers spreads on the wind. But others rely on insects such as bees and butterflies, or even birds and bats to help them spread their pollen. Bright colors draw the bees to the flower's sweet juice or nectar. As they sip it, they brush the stamens and pick up pollen which they carry to the next flower they sip.

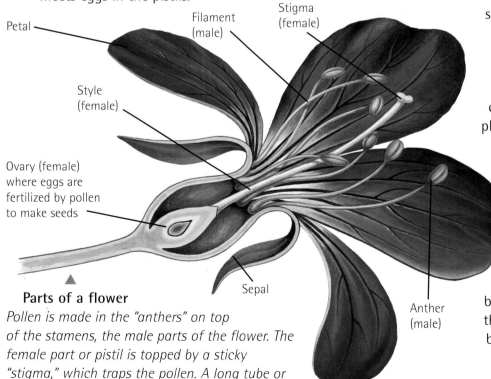

Petal

Filament (male)

Stigma (female)

Style (female)

Ovary (female) where eggs are fertilized by pollen to make seeds

Sepal

Anther (male)

▲ **Parts of a flower**
*Pollen is made in the "anthers" on top of the stamens, the male parts of the flower. The female part or pistil is topped by a sticky "stigma," which traps the pollen. A long tube or "style" takes it down to the ovary where it meets the eggs to create the seeds.*

Waxwing

Jay

### ◀ Seed spreaders
*Some seeds are spread by the wind in feathery seed cases. But many are spread by insects, birds and other animals. Birds such as these eat fruits, drawn by their color. They digest the flesh, but the hard seed passes through the bird and emerges ready for germination.*

## Are fruits seeds?

No, they develop from the flower's ovary—and the hard pips inside are the seeds. Juicy fruits such as berries are called "true fruits" because they are made from the flower's ovaries alone. Apples and pears are "false" fruits because only the core is made from the ovary. Plums and cherries are "drupes" meaning there are no pips, but the seed is held in a hard shell.

## Are any vegetables fruits?

Potatoes and other root vegetables are plant roots, not seeds. But peas, beans, and other "legumes" are actually fruit and the seeds are the peas and beans inside the pod.

## How do seeds grow?

Each seed is the germ (start) of a new plant and contains the food it needs to help it germinate (grow into a plant). Growth starts with just a single root or radicle, which grows down into the soil, and a single green shoot, or plumule, which grows up toward the sun. Then the plant's seed leaves—its first leaves, like baby teeth— appear. Soon after, the main stem begins to grow, and true leaves sprout from this.

### ▶ Date palm
*The sweet, sticky fruit of the date palm looks a little like a plum, but it is not a drupe. The stone of a date is actually the seed for a new tree, not the seed container like the plum stone.*

# QUIZ

1  How many pollen grains can a single American ragweed make in a day: a) 18 b) 1,800 c) 18 billion?

2  The flowers of the baobab tree are pollinated by bushbabies: true or false?

3  How many seeds can a single flower of the trumpet tree of the Amazon rain forest make: a) 900 b) 900,000 c) 9 million?

4  Are any seeds poisonous?

5  Do any flowers bloom just for a day?

6  What are the smallest seeds?

7  What are the world's oldest flowers?

**Answers**
1. c) 2. True 3. b) 4. Yes, to save them being eaten by birds 5. Yes, like morning glory and the day lily 6. Orchids 7. Magnolias

# Trees and shrubs

## What are trees?

**A**LTHOUGH SOME DWARF WILLOWS are just a few inches high, most trees are much bigger; trees are the biggest of all plants. The biggest trees are the world's biggest living things, as tall as a skyscraper. They can grow big because they have huge numbers of leaves and hard, woody stems covered in a protective layer of bark.

## What are conifers?

Conifers, are among the oldest of all plants, first appearing more than 275 million years ago. They get their name from the fact that they rely on cones rather than flowers to make the seeds for new trees. They usually grow tall and straight with hardly any big side branches and, unlike "broad-leaved" trees, they tend to have narrow, needle-like leaves.

## What is an evergreen?

An evergreen is a tree that keeps its leaves all the year round. Each leaf lasts for years, and is usually a dark, waxy green. The leaves of trees that lose their leaves each year, called deciduous trees, are a lighter, yellow green.

### ▶ Going red

*As days grow shorter and colder in autumn, the chlorophyll which makes leaves green breaks down in deciduous trees like the maple. This allows other colours — yellows, reds, browns and golds — to shine through, giving the trees their beautiful autumn hues.*

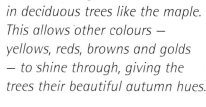

## Why do some trees lose their leaves every year?

Deciduous trees such as oaks, ashes, and elms shed their leaves to cut down on moisture loss in seasons when water is harder to come by. In the tropics, they lose their leaves at the start of the dry season. In temperate regions, between the tropics and the poles, they lose them in autumn because water is much harder to come by in winter.

## Why don't all trees lose their leaves?

In warm, moist places, like tropical rain forests, moisture is available all year round, so even broad-leaved trees can keep their leaves all year round. Conifers, too, can keep their leaves, because their narrow needles do not lose moisture nearly as quickly as the big leaves of broad-leaved trees, so they can survive through the winter when water is short.

## What are tree rings?

If a tree is cut across the trunk, you can see the trunk is marked by a series of rings called growth rings. These show how the tree has grown each year. The edge of the ring marks where growth ceased in winter. By counting the rings, you can tell how old a tree is. You can also tell whether a summer was good or bad for tree growth from just how wide each of the rings is.

## What is heartwood?

Heartwood is the dark, dense dead wood found in the center of a tree trunk. It is surrounded by lighter, living "sapwood," which carries all the tubes that feed moisture and nourishment to the tree's leaves.

Jay

▶ **Life in a tree**
*An oak tree like this is home to countless animals and plants. Birds nest on branches and in holes, insects feed on the leaves and burrow in the bark, and fungi and ivy grow on the trunk.*

Tawny owl

Woodpecker

Stag beetle

Ivy

Bracket fungi

# QUIZ

1  The giant sequoia tree in California is the world's biggest living thing. Is it a) 138 feet (42m) b) 272 feet (83m) c) 505 feet (154m)?

2  Every tree can be identified by its leaves: true or false?

3  What tree is the national symbol of Canada?

4  What is the seed of the oak tree called?

5  Can trees warn other trees of caterpillar attacks?

6  Is the eucalyptus of Tasmania commonly known as a a) gum tree b) oil tree c) glue tree?

7  Are the pipes that carry a tree's sap called a) reeds b) xylem c) xylophones?

15

# Plants for food

## What food do plants give?

**P**LANTS GIVE most of the world's people their "staple" food, the basic food they need for survival–whether it is bread, or cereal or soybeans. Fruit and vegetables provide us with most of the vitamins we need to keep us healthy. They also make some of the most delicious foods and drinks, from apple pies to orange juice.

### Why do we eat grass?

Cereals are the world's most important foods—including wheat, rice, corn, barley, oats, and rye—and they are all grasses. We usually eat their seeds, or "grain," leaving the stalks and leaves to rot to make silage to feed animals.

### What is wheat?

Wheat is the most important of the cereals. It was first cultivated in the Middle East 12,000 years ago from the wild grass emmer. Now it provides the basic food for more than a third of the world's population. Wheat grain is usually ground into flour to make bread and pasta and many other things.

### What was the Green Revolution?

40 years ago, farmers in North America and Europe began growing special "high-yield" varieties of wheat, rice, and corn. These grow so fast and big they give bumper harvests—sometimes more than twice a year. Soon, the idea was adopted in India and elsewhere.

### What's wrong with the Green Revolution?

High-yield crops only give big harvests if the land is well watered and the farmer uses a lot of fertilizer, pesticides, and machines—farmers now need to apply ten times as much nitrogen fertilizer to keep the soil fertile as they did 40 years ago. This not only poses much greater strains on the environment, but means small farmers may be put in debt to the suppliers of fertilizers, pesticides, and seeds.

### What are root crops?

Root crops are plants cultivated mainly for their big, solid roots, such as potatoes, yams, cassava and manioc. These roots are rich in carbohydrates, the food we need for energy.

▶ **Paddy fields**

*In Asia, most people's basic food is rice, grown in flooded fields called paddies, where they can grow up to three crops a year. To keep the fields flooded on steep hillsides, farmers often have to build row upon row of terraces.*

▲ **Corn fed**

*Corn is usually grown on large farms. It comes in two main forms. One has a big head with big grains and gives us corn on the cob and sweetcorn (above). The other has a small head and small grains and gives us corn oil and corn starch.*

## Where does chocolate come from?

Chocolate is made with cocoa powder, ground up from the roasted and fermented beans of cacao pods. The pods are the fruit of the cacao tree, which came originally from the Andes mountains in South America, but is now grown mainly in West Africa and the Caribbean.

## How many plants can be eaten?

There are more than 12,000 species of edible plant, but fewer than 100 are usually grown as crops.

## Which plants give sugar

Most sugar came originally from the sweet sap of sugarcane, a tall grass that grows in the tropics, especially the Caribbean. Now as much comes from the sweet, thick roots of sugarbeet, a plant that grows well in cooler places.

▲ Prickly pear
*Different crops grow well in different places. In the hottest, driest parts of India, farmers often grow this cactus, called a prickly pear, which yields a sweet fruit.*

Some rice terraces, like these in the Philippines, are thousands of years old

Most paddy rice is still planted and picked by hand

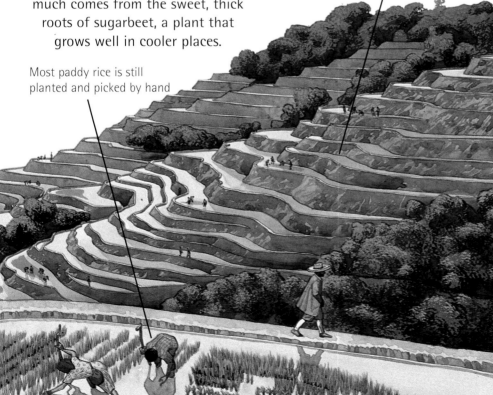

# QUIZ

1  Is a fallow: a) an old Irishman b) a kind of fruit c) a period in which soil is allowed to rest and recover?

2  Is a cash crop: a) an expensive haircut b) a banker's whip c) a crop a farmer grows to sell for money, not to eat?

3  What is a combine harvester?

4  Where did potatoes come from originally: a) Ireland b) South America c) India?

5  What plant gives most of our wine?

6  Japanese farmers use 65 times as much fertilizer per acre on their grains as farmers in Nigeria: true or false?

Answers
1. c) 2. c) 3. A machine which both cuts the wheat from the ground and separates the grain from the stalks 4. b) 5. The grape vine 6. True

# Plants for health

## Can plants heal?

YES. PLANTS HAVE BEEN USED as medicines since prehistoric times, and the effectiveness of some is beyond doubt. Many of today's most important drugs, such as aspirin, morphine, and quinine, came originally from plants. In some countries such as China, herbal remedies are still among the most widely used of all medicines, although not all are equally effective.

### ▲ Poppy power

*The opium poppy is the source of opium, which oozes from the unripe seed head when cut with a knife. Opium is the source of the powerful drug morphine, used to help ease extreme pain. It is the basis too for the milder painkiller codeine, used in cough medicines. Opium can also be turned into the dangerously addictive drug heroin, which is why it is sometimes grown in secret in Southeast Asia.*

### ▶ Plants for health: key
1. *Periwinkle*
2. *Feverfew*
3. *White willow*
4. *Opium poppy*
5. *Foxglove*

### How can a willow cure a headache?

People used to chew willow bark to ease pain. In the last century, scientists discovered this worked because willow contains a certain chemical, also found in meadowsweet. This chemical was later used to make aspirin.

### Why might a foxglove stop your heart?

Foxglove in large doses is highly poisonous. But it also yields the drug digitalis, used in small doses to treat heart problems.

### Can plants cure cancer?

No drug yet known can cure cancer. But an extract of the rosy periwinkle, vincristine, is very effective against leukemia, the childhood cancer.

## Why might a gin and tonic help cure malaria?

The tropical disease malaria once killed millions of people. Then it was discovered that it could be treated with quinine, extracted from the bark of South America's cinchona tree. Quinine also gives the bitter flavor in tonic water.

## How did feverfew get its name?

"Feverfew" comes from the plant's Latin name *febrifuga*, which means driving away fever, and it was once thought an effective treatment of fever. It is still used to alleviate headaches today.

## What is ginseng?

Ginseng is a plant related to ivy, prized in China for 5,000 years. Its powdered root helps relieve tiredness, and is said to relieve kidney disease and headaches.

## Why did women put deadly nightshade in their eyes?

Deadly nightshade has poisonous, red berries. The juice of these berries is used to make the drug atropine, which makes the pupil bigger for eye examinations. In the Middle Ages, women put this juice in their eyes to make their pupils wider and more attractive, which is why the plant is also called "belladonna," from the Italian for beautiful woman.

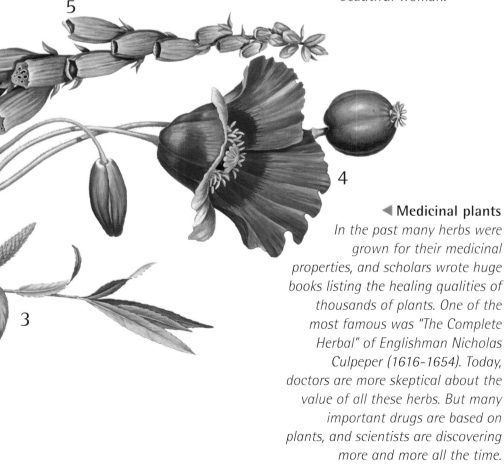

5

4

3

◀ **Medicinal plants**
*In the past many herbs were grown for their medicinal properties, and scholars wrote huge books listing the healing qualities of thousands of plants. One of the most famous was "The Complete Herbal" of Englishman Nicholas Culpeper (1616-1654). Today, doctors are more skeptical about the value of all these herbs. But many important drugs are based on plants, and scientists are discovering more and more all the time.*

# QUIZ

1 Oranges are good for preventing colds: true or false?

2 The coca in Coca-Cola is the same coca plant that the dangerous drug cocaine comes from: true or false?

3 Coffee beans contain the stimulating drug caffeine: true or false?

4 Is someone who studies plant medicine: a) a vegetarian b) a herbalist c) a plantain?

5 The wild yam—a bit like a turnip—helps with birth control: true or false?

6 Poison ivy is a type of clover: true or false?

7 Rubbing beet on the skin cures acne: true or false?

8 Lungwort gets its name because it is good for lung problems: true or false?

**Answers**
1. True 2. True; Coca-cola originally contained coca and cola, a nut that contains the pick-me-up caffeine 3. True 4. b) 5. True 6. False 7. False — but it makes all your face equally red! 8. True

# Plants for materials

## What kinds of materials can plants be used for?

**P**LANTS PROVIDE A HUGE range of materials, used for all kinds of purposes. The most important is wood for building and paper, perhaps, but there is also cotton for clothes, cork for wine bottles, oils, rubber, dyes, rope and string, and much more besides.

### ▲ Cotton head

*Many of our clothes are made from cotton—or cotton mixed with man-made fibers. Cotton is a natural fiber that comes from the cotton flower, a plant that grows in warm regions. Its seed pods or "bolls" hold a dense mass of fluffy fibers, which can be separated into strands of cotton "lint." It is the lint from which cotton cloth is woven.*

### What plants make paper?

Most paper is made from wood pulped into a soft white mush. Many conifers are planted especially for paper. But natural forests are also a source. The main trees are spruce and pine, but aspen, poplar, and eucalyptus are used too. In south Asia, paper may be made from bamboo. Paper can also be made from grasses, straw, and sugarcane.

### What trees make wood?

All trees are woody, but we call wood for making things from timber. Timber is either softwood or hardwood. Softwood comes from fast-growing conifers like pine, larch, fir, and spruce, which grow in colder places. Hardwood is from slow-growing, broad-leaved trees such as oak. It also comes from tropical trees like mahogany.

### ▲ Reed hut

*In the past, people made the most of plants that were available locally. Some of the first boats and houses were made from reeds pulled from marshes. The Ancient Egyptians and South Americans made boats of weed. The Marsh Arabs of southern Iraq still do.*

### ▶ Wooden houses

*When most European people still lived in the countryside, before the Industrial Revolution of 200 years ago, only the houses of the very rich were built mainly of brick or stone. Most ordinary houses were built with timber frames and even walls, and were often roofed by thatches made from reeds and straw.*

## ▶ Plant carrier

*When tankers carry oil, the fuel we use to run cars and fire power stations, they are in fact carrying the ancient remains of plants and animals.*

# QUIZ

1 How do plants give plastics?

2 Where does mahogany come from?

3 What plant is sunflower oil made from?

4 Cork comes from the sea: true or false?

5 Does ivory come from a plant or an animal?

6 What connects bicycle wheels with tropical plants?

7 What color dye did Ancient Britons make from the leaves of the yellow flower woad?

8 Why does a madder plant make you redder?

## What are fossil fuels?

Fossil fuels are fuels such as coal, oil, and natural gas, made mainly from the remains of plants that died long ago. The remains were buried underground and gradually squeezed and concentrated into fuels over millions of years. Coal was made from giant ferns that grew in huge swamps 300 million years ago; oil from tiny plants and animals that lived in warm seas.

## How do plants warm houses and run cars?

Plants provide 80% of all our fuels— for running cars, keeping houses, warm and generating power. In developing countries, most people cook and keep warm by burning wood they gather from forests and shrubs. In Brazil, they run cars not on gasoline but on a fuel like diesel, tapped from the copaiba tree. In North America and many other places in the world, the main fuels are fossil fuel—that is, coal, oil, and natural gas.

Answers

1. Most plastics are made from either oil or coal 2. Tropical rain forests 3. The seeds of the sunflower 4. False; cork comes the bark of the cork-oak tree 5. Animal; the elephant 6. The tires are made of rubber which comes originally from the sap of the rubber tree 7. Blue 8. Madder is a flower which gives a red dye

# Woodland plants

## What are woodland plants?

WOODLANDS are the home for plants that prefer the shady conditions under trees to full sunlight. There are spring flowers such as bluebells and primroses, summer flowers such as foxgloves and rosebay willowherb, shrubs such as brambles and hawthorn, as well as ferns, mosses, and fungi.

▼ **Woodland plants**

*This picture shows just some of the many wildflowers and other plants that grow on the woodland floor. Although all the flowers are shown in bloom here, they do not all bloom at the same time. Each has its season, keeping the floor alive with color for many months of the year.*

## Why do primroses bloom in spring?

Like many flowers of deciduous woodlands, primroses bloom in spring before the leaves have grown thick on the trees, so that they get plenty of sunshine. Many other woodland flowers bloom in spring for the same reason, including wood anemones, oxlips, daffodils, lesser celandines, bluebells, early purple orchids, and dog's mercury. It is flowers like these that give the woodland floor a colorful carpet every spring.

## Why are dead trees good news?

When big trees die and come crashing down through the branches, they creating a clearing in the wood called a glade. Here sunlight can reach the woodland floor again, allowing all kinds of plants to sprout anew, including flowers such as foxgloves and rosebay willowherb and all kinds of fungi, such as fly agaric, which thrive on the rotting wood.

## What plant has two different flowers?

Wood sorrel has a big spring flower to attract the bees that spread its pollen, and another smaller flower in summer to make seeds.

◄ **Woodland plants: key**
1. Lords and ladies
2. Wood anemones
3. Honeysuckle
4. Fly agaric
5. Wood Blewit
6. Bluebells
7. Orchid
8. Primrose
9. Rhododendron

## Which woodland plant is good for a kiss?

At Christmas, many people still hang up a sprig of mistletoe and kiss beneath it. Mistletoe is a parasitic plant with white berries which clings to trees such as apples, hawthorns, poplars, and willows and puts its roots into them. The custom goes back to the druids, the white-robed priests of Ancient Britain more than 2,000 years ago, who used to cut down mistletoe with a golden sickle to use in their sacred rites.

## What is a coppice?

Since early times, people living in woodland areas have cut down trees to allow new, straight shoots to grow through. This is called coppicing, and ensured a good supply of straight poles for fencing and making tools.

## Are fruits seeds?

No, they develop from the flower's ovary—and the hard pips inside are the seeds. Juicy fruits such as berries are called "true fruits" because they are made from the flower's ovaries alone. Apples and pears are "false" fruits because only the core is made from the ovary. Plums and cherries are "drupes" in which there are no pips, but the seed is held in a hard shell.

# QUIZ

1 What poison do foxgloves contain a) arsenic b) cyanide c) digitalis?

2 What trees are used to make baseball bats?

3 King Alfred's cake fungus gets its name because it looks like burned buns: true or false?

4 What is a bloody cranesbill?

5 Fungus sharpens knives: true or false?

6 In spring, the faint ringing of bluebells can be heard in woods: true or false?

7 Elizabethan lords used lords and ladies for a) cooking b) stiffening their collars c) smoking?

8 Ferns are the world's oldest trees: true or false?

**Answers**
1. c) 2. Hickory 3. True 4. A crimson flower 5. True; the razor strop fungus was used to sharpen razors 6. False 7. b) 8. True; there were forests of ferns 300 million years ago

23

# Tropical plants

## What makes tropical plants different?

THE TROPICS ARE WARM nearly all the time, and in the rain forests there is abundant moisture. The combination creates almost ideal conditions for plant growth, and the forests are not only lush but contain an astonishing variety of plants–including some of the world's most spectacular and strange.

▲ The Rafflesia has no leaves, and the only part of the plant above ground is the huge, blotchy red and white bloom. It is a parasite, and beneath the ground is a tangle of thread-like roots growing inside the roots of lianas and gaining nourishment from them.

### What is the world's biggest flower?

A single bloom of the Rafflesia of Southeast Asia can be 3 feet (90cm) across and weigh 15 pounds (7kg) or more. The titan arum is 10 feet (3m) tall, but is made of many small flowers, not asingle bloom like Rafflesia.

### What is the world's worst smelling flower?

The Rafflesia may not only be the world's biggest flower; it may also be the foulest smelling. Some people call it the stinking corpse lily and say it smells like rotting meat. The stench is said to draw the flies it needs to pollinate.

### How many plants are there in the rain forest?

The rain forests are the world's richest habitats, containing over 40 percent of all plant species. No one knows exactly how many different plants there are, but botanists counted more than 180 species of tree alone in one hectare (2.4 acres) of the Malaysian forest.

### Do plants grow on trees?

The forest is so dense that to get nearer sunlight, small plants called epiphytes wrap their roots around high branches and grow there. The most common epiphytes are bromeliads.

### What is the strongest rope in the jungle?

The liana is a vine or creeper that dangles down from trees in the rain forest. It is so strong that monkeys and other forest animals can use lianas to swing through the trees. The vine is actually a very long stem. The liana's roots are in the ground and its leaves are in the sun above the trees.

### What are the world's largest leaves?

Palm tree leaves can be very big. The leaves of raffia palms and the Amazonian bamboo palm can grow up to 65 feet (20m) long.

▶ What makes the rain forest so rich in plant life is that plants don't just grow in the soil. Trees are festooned not only with dangling creepers and vines, but many plants that actually grow in the tree, including bromeliads, orchids, ferns, and mosses—and "air plants," which get enough moisture from the air alone.

## What plants have their own water tanks?

Some bromeliads grow high up on trees and their roots cannot reach water from the ground. Instead, they grow a tight cluster of leaves which traps a pond of rainwater.

## What are the layers in a tropical forest?

The top layer is the "emergent" layer—a few trees, towering above the rest, up to 200 feet (60m) tall. Beneath them, 100-150 feet (30-50m) above the ground, is the dense "canopy" of leaves and branches of big trees. In the gloom beneath is the "understory" where small trees and shrubs grow.

## Why are rain forests threatened?

Every year an area of rain forest the size of Belgium is burned or cut down to make way for grazing land—or simply for the wood. Once cut down, it takes centuries to grow again—if it ever does—because the forest's richness lies not in the soil, which is easily washed away once exposed, but in the trees themselves.

# QUIZ

1 Is the world's biggest rain forest in a) Brazil b) India c) Australia?

2 The world's fastest growing plant is Burma's giant bamboo. In a day, it can grow a) 1 inch (2.5cm) b) 7 inches (17cm) c) 18 inches (46cm)?

3 Flowers grow on tree trunks in the jungle: true or false?

4 There is a plant in the jungle that eats frogs: true or false?

5 There is a plant in the jungle that strangles trees: true or false?

6 There are exploding cucumbers in the jungle: true or false?

7 Lianas can strangle monkeys: true or false?

**Answers**
1. a) 2. c) 3. True 4. True; the venus flytrap does 5. True; the strangler fig does 6. True; the squirting cucumber shoots seeds up to 26 feet (8m) 7. False; except by accident

# Water plants

## What plants grow in water?

The very first plants developed in water, then gradually colonized the land as they evolved. Since then many new plants–called aquatic plants–have learned to live in water, including flowers like water lilies, water hyacinths, and grass-like plants such as reeds, rushes, and papyrus.

### Do plants float?

Yes, the leaves of flowers like the water lily and hyacinth float on the surface. But the leaves are on long, flexible stalks that reach down to the lake or riverbed, and the roots are firmly anchored in the mud. Even so, they cannot survive in fast-moving water.

### Why don't floating plants sink?

Because some plants have air sacks in their stems and leaves. Others, like the water lily, have leaves that turn up at the edges so that they float like boats.

### What is the world's biggest water plant?

The leaves of the giant lily of the Amazon in South America grow 6 feet (1.8m) across and can bear the weight of a child.

### What water plant did the Pharaohs write on?

The papyrus is a giant reed that grows along the River Nile. The Ancient Egyptians discovered 5,000 years ago that the pith of papyrus stems could be used to make paper. Although paper is now made from wood pulp, we owe the word to the papyrus reed.

### Why are water hyacinths a nuisance?

The purple flowers of the floating water hyacinth are attractive, but the plants can spread rapidly, choking waterways and blocking the path of boats.

## How do river plants cope with the current?

To survive in anything but the very slowest-flowing rivers, water plants have to anchor themselves with firm roots to save themselves from being washed away, and their leaves must be feathery, like those of the fanwort, to avoid offering resistance to the water. The river water crowfoot can survive in quite fast-flowing streams because its leaves are streamlined.

## What water plant eats bugs?

The bladderwort is a plant of swamps that develops underwater bladders on its stem. When an insect such as a water flea touches a trigger on one of these bladders, the bladder springs open and sucks in the flea with the inrushing water.

## Why don't all lakes have plants?

Because the chemical composition of the water varies. Lakes filled by water draining from lime-rich soils tend to to be rich in plant life. Those near acid soil are more sterile.

### ▼ Water life

*Slow-flowing rivers and shallows in lakes are often densely packed with all kinds of water plants. Most plants are rooted to the bed, but a few get all the nutrients they need directly from the water. Some plants are hidden underwater. Some float on the surface. Plants such as rushes and reeds are called emergents because they grow up out of the water.*

**Key**: *1. Bulrushes 2. Frogbit 3. Water crowfoot 4. Water lily 5. Yellow flag iris 6. Water plantain*

# QUIZ

1 What water flower was adopted as a symbol by French and English kings?

2 What important food crop is grown in water in China?

3 Do lakes last forever?

4 How do water plants keep out the rain in parts of England?

5 The Amazonian Indians make cartwheels out of water-lily leaves: true or false?

6 What water plants did the Egyptians make boats from?

7 What water plants was Moses found among?

8 The pollen of most water plants spreads by floating on the water: true or false?

**Answers**
1. The yellow flag iris or fleur-de-lys 2. Rice 3. No, most are eventually choked by plants and silt 4. Sedges are used for thatching rooves 5. False 6. Reed 7. Bulrushes, though the famous Victorian painting by Alma-Tadema wrongly shows reedmace 8. True

# Grassland plants

## Are grasslands all grass?

**A**T FIRST GLANCE grasslands look as uniform and unvaried as a lawn-just mile upon mile of green grass. But a closer look reveals that there are, for a start, many types of grass, including tussock grass, marram grass, meadow grass, blue grass, and many more-and mixed in with the grasses are a rich variety of herbs and flowers.

**▲ Rokerboom**
*There is too little water for most ordinary trees in tropical grasslands like the veld of South Africa. So, like the baobab of the savanna, the rokerboom tree has developed a huge swollen trunk that acts as a water store to help it survive through dry periods.*

**▼ South American pampas**
*The pampas stretches across Argentina, Uruguay, and southeastern Brazil, forming the largest area of temperate grassland in the southern hemisphere. Many parts of the pampas are dominated by tussock grasses like those seen in the foreground.*

### Do grasslands have any other name?
They have special names in every continent. In North America they are called prairies. In South America, they are called pampas. In northern Asia, they are the steppes. In South Africa, they are the veld. In Australia, the bush. In Britain, grasslands occur mostly on chalk hills and are called downs.

### Where do grasslands occur?
Grasslands occur all over the world where there is only moderate rainfall—mostly in the heart of continents, far from the sea—or where the ground is so dry and well-drained that only grass will grow.

### Why don't trees grow in grasslands?
Because trees need a lot of water. Grasslands are too dry. The few trees that do grow in grasslands, such as the baobab and the rokerboom, have immensely thick trunks that are very good at retaining moisture.

### What is meadow grass?
Meadow grass is the most common of all grasses, found in grasslands all over the world. This is the grass that people use in lawns. It is almost always green because although each plant lasts only a few years, they continually produce fresh seeds, so new grass is springing up all the time.

► **Acacias**

*Acacia trees, sometimes known as thorn trees because of their prickly thorns, are the most widespread trees of the African savanna, and their flat tops are a distinctive part of the savanna landscape. Their partnership with ants helps them survive. The acacia's leaf stalks secrete a nectar, which attracts ants. In return, the ants attack any animal that tries to browse on the leaves. They also help to spread the acacia's seeds.*

## Why do farmers like rye grass?

Rye grass is the grass that many farmers grow for cows to graze on, and to make hay for feeding livestock from. Typically, new pastures are sown with either pure rye grass or mixed rye and clover.

## What wild flowers grow on grasslands?

Vetches, trefoils, worts, orchids, and various herbs are among the many flowers native to grasslands.

## Which garden flowers come from grasslands?

Flowers from the prairies of North America include the coneflower, the sunflower, and the blazing star. From the grasslands of Europe and Asia come flowers such as adonis, anemones, delphiniums, and scabious.

## How did scabious get its name?

The juice was said to cure scabies and other skin diseases.

# QUIZ

1 What animals are raised on the pampas?

2 What large animal used to roam the prairies?

3 What animals are raised on Australian grasslands?

4 Which U.S. state is famous for its bluegrass a) California b) South Carolina c) Kentucky?

5 What is a billabong?

6 What color is prairie soil a) brown b) black c) yellow?

7 On which continent would you find a gaucho?

8 What is a big cattle farm on the prairies called?

9 What was a prairie schooner?

10 What grass would you find on sand dunes a) sedge grass b) rye grass c) marram grass?

# Desert plants

## Do any plants grow in the desert?

**A** DESERT IS A PLACE where very little rain falls–but only rarely is there no rain at all, and wherever there is a little moisture, some especially adapted hardy plants, such as cacti, will survive.

### How do plants find water in the desert?

When there is no water on the surface, plants can often find moisture deep underground by growing long roots. Mesquite roots grow as deep as 30 feet (9m), and may be 150 feet (43m) deep.

### How do plants save water?

Wherever water is short, plants have developed ways of saving water. Other plants lose a great deal of water by evaporation from their leaves. So desert plants usually have tough, waxy leaves— and plants that live in extreme conditions cut down their leaves to a minimum.

▶ **Saguaro**
*The saguaro of the southwest states and Mexico is the biggest cactus, growing up to 60 feet (18m) tall and 2 feet (60cm) thick.*

### What plant amputates its own branches?

The branches and trunk of the quiver tree are filled with a soft fiber that can store water. But in severe drought, it seals off branches to save moisture loss through the leaves. The branch end looks like an amputated limb.

▲ Oasis
*In places in the Sahara desert in Africa, water-bearing rocks are exposed at the surface, creating an oasis where moisture-loving plants such as palm trees can flourish.*

▼ **Cactus in flower**
*Cacti have to pollinate just like every other flowering plant and so every few years they produce big colourful blooms in order to attract insects quickly.*

### What is a window plant?
Some plants, such as pebble plants, escape the drying heat of the desert by growing partly underground. But the window plant grows almost entirely underground. It is like a cigar poked down into the ground. All that is visible on the surface is the end, a little green button—the plant's window to the sun.

### How do cacti survive in Death Valley?
Cacti are the most impressive of all desert survivors. They are remarkable plants that live in American deserts. They have no leaves and a very thick skin, so water loss is cut to a minimum. Their fat stems are able to hold huge quantities of water, which is why they are called succulents.

### Why is cactus prickly?
Lush vegetation is so rare in the desert that animals eat anything available. So plants such as cacti, prickly pears, and thorn bushes, grow prickles to protect themselves from being eaten.

◄ **Blooms in the desert**
*When it rains in the desert, seeds that have lain dormant during the long drought suddenly burst into brief bloom.*
**Key**: *1. Saguaro 2. Evening primrose 3. Prickly pear*

3

# QUIZ

1  Is a half-man a) a mythical camel b) a desert monkey c) a prickly desert plant?

2  How much does the Joshua tree of the Mojave Desert grow in a year: a) 0.5 inch (1cm) b) 4 inches (10cm) c) 40 inches (100cm)?

3  What happens to the shriveled brown leaves of a resurrection tree after it rains?

4  Where do some owls live in the deserts?

5  What is the hottest desert?

6  How often does it rain in Chile's Atacama desert—every a) 5 years b) 20 years c) 400 years?

**Answers**
1. c) 2. b) 3. The leaves turn green 4. In holes in cacti 5. The Sahara, where it often gets to 110°F (43°C) 6. c)

31

# Mountain plants

## What plants live on mountains?

THE WEATHER GETS COLDER, windier, and wetter the higher you go up a mountain. Some mountaintops are even permanently covered with snow. So the plants that grow on mountains have to be hardy, and they usually get smaller the higher you go, varying from big trees such as conifers on the lower slopes to tiny flowers, low grasses, and mosses higher up.

▼ Alpine flowers: key
1. Alpine bluebell 2. Alpine gentian
3. Mountain avens 4. Edelweiss
5. Purple saxifrage

## What is the timber line?

Above a certain height, it gets too cold for trees to grow well. This is the timber line. It varies according to local conditions, but gets lower toward the poles. It is about 9,200 feet (2,800m) in the Alps.

## Can plants survive on rock faces?

The purple saxifrage and starry saxifrage have tough, penetrating roots that exploit cracks and crevices, enabling them to colonize the narrowest rocky ledges. Their roots anchor so firmly that they were once thought to be able to actually crack the rock. The word saxifrage means "stone breaker."

## Why do some alpine flowers have big blooms?

There are few insects to pollinate flowers high up on the mountainside, so flowers such as purple saxifrage and the snow gentian produce big colorful blooms to ensure that insects don't waste time searching for them.

▶ Edelweiss
*The edelweiss can grow at very high altitudes in the Alps, sprouting out from cracks in the rocks, because its blooms and leaves are covered in a coat of wooly hairs that protect it from the cold.*

## How do alpine flowers cope with a short summer?

High up near the snowline, the time available for growing after the snow melts in spring is very short. So the alpine snowbell makes the most of each summer by developing its flowerbuds the previous summer. They lie dormant through the winter under a protective blanket of snow, ready to burst through at the first thaw.

## How do plants survive in the cold ?

Plants have evolved various different ways of coping with the cold. Some cover themselves with a coat of wooly hairs, like edelweiss, or have thick, waxy leaves. The Himalayan saussurea is almost all wool. Others, such as the daisies of Tasmania, pack their stems into a tight padded cushion.

## Can plants freeze?

Few plants can survive being frozen, but many can thrive under the snow. Snow acts like a blanket, keeping ice and wind at bay, and saves the plant from being frozen to death. Alpine grasses stay alive and green under the snow, ready to grow again as soon as it melts.

## Where are there dandelions as big as trees?

On Mt. Kenya in Africa, baking daytime sun and icy nights have created giant groundsels. Elsewhere, groundsel is a small plant similar to dandelions—but on Mt. Kenya it grows more than 30 feet (9m) tall! The European lobelia is a tiny plant too—but on Mt. Kenya, lobelias grow huge.

◀ Alpine flowers
*Above the timber line, many small flowers thrive, including cinquefoil, stonecrop, and campion, besides those shown.*

5

33

# Arctic plants

## Do plants grow in the Arctic?

**F**OR NINE MONTHS of the year, the Arctic is bitterly cold and dark. But for a few months in summer, it is daylight most of the time, and in this brief respite from the worst of Arctic weather, a surprising variety of plants–more than 900 species–spring up.

### Why does it never get dark in the Arctic summer?

In summer, the sun sets for only a few hours in the middle of the night. This happens because the Earth is tilted over. As the Earth makes its year-long journey round the Sun, the part of the Earth tilted toward the Sun gradually shifts north, then south. In the Arctic summer, the Earth has reached the point in its journey where the North Pole is tilting most toward the Sun.

### Why are trees shorter than daisies?

Willow trees grow in the Arctic, but because of the fierce Arctic wind, they never grow more than 4 inches (10cm) tall. Instead, they spread out along the ground.

### Why do Arctic plants like skulls?

Nutriment is so scarce in the Arctic that plants take what there is. So when an animal such as a musk ox dies, seeds make the most of its corpse, and Arctic flowers often spring up inside the skull.

### How do some plants melt snow?

Some plants have dark leaves and stems. When the sun shines, their dark color soaks up the sun's warmth and melts the snow.

▶ **Arctic bloom: key**
1. *Saxifrage*
2. *Snowbell*
3. *Avens*
4. *Willowherb*
5. *Saxifrage*
6. *Stonecrop*
7. *Arctic poppy*

## How do plants cope without bees to pollinate them?

There are so few bees and butterflies in the Arctic that many Arctic flowers find other ways of spreading their pollen. Some flowers, like mustard, rely on the wind. Others rely on flies, and so only put out yellow or white flowers, since flies are color blind.

## What is the tundra?

Tundra is a region so cold that no large trees grow—only dwarf trees, shrubs such as heathers, grasses, and other small plants. There is a vast area of tundra stretching through the north of Canada, Siberia, and Scandinavia and into Greenland. There is tundra on high mountains too.

## Why are many Arctic plants evergreen?

Leaves grown the previous summer are ready to make the most of the brief summer. Over the winter, they are protected by dead leaves.

## Do plants grow in Antarctica?

Most of Antarctica is covered in snow and ice all year round, so very few plants can survive here, unlike the Arctic. Yet there are fungi and lichen growing within 300 miles (500km) of the South Pole, and two species of flowering plant are native to Antarctica.

## Why is snow pink in Antarctica?

Some algae live in the snow, just below the surface, but the UV rays from the sun are so bright in snow that the algae must protect itself with red pigment. The red algae turns the snow pink.

◀ Arctic bloom

*Full-size trees will not grow in the Arctic tundra, but the brief summer sees it bursting into life. Grasses and sedges, mosses and lichens thrive, along with various small flowers such as saxifrages, avens, and Arctic poppies, especially adapted to survive the cold.*

6

7

# QUIZ

1  Gentian is used to make a bitter tonic for stomach complaints—true or false?

2  Which flower blooms nearest the North Pole a) snowdrop b) bluebell c) Arctic poppy?

3  Lichen growing in Antarctica may be the world's oldest living things. Are they a) 1,000 years old b) 10,000 years old c) 100,000 years old?

4  In Antarctica, the temperature can drop to a) 5°F (-15°C) b) -128°F (-89°C) c) -423°F (-253°C)?

5  Is the North Pole in the Arctic or Antarctic?

**Answers**
1. True  2. c)  3. b)  4. b)
5. The Arctic

What creature turns green with rage?

Why do elephants have trunks?

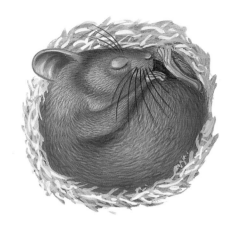

How do seals keep warm?

Why does a woodpecker peck wood?

Which bird never sees the sunset?

Why does a beaver slap its tail on the water?

What's the noisiest creature in the Amazon jungle?

What frog makes Indian arrows deadly?

Why is a flamingo pink?

What bird has a beak as big as its body?

# Animals

Do bears hug?

How does a giraffe drink?

What is a female deer called?

# Rain-forest animals

## What animals live in rain forests?

THE LUSH, WARM RAIN FORESTS of the tropics are home to more species of animal than any other habitat in the world. Huge numbers of small, tree-dwelling creatures especially live here–scores of different reptiles such as snakes and lizards, hundreds of different kinds of bird, and perhaps more than a million different insects.

### What creature turns green with rage?

The chameleon is a strange tree lizard with swivelling eyes, a long tail that coils up and an amazingly long sticky tongue that darts out to catch flies. But what is strangest of all is that the chameleon can change its skin color, either when it is in a certain mood—in a rage, for instance—or to camouflage itself by blending in perfectly with its background.

### What frog makes Indian arrows deadly?

The sweat of the poison-arrow tree frogs of Central and South America is deadly to humans. Local Indians collect the poison by holding the frogs over a fire to make them sweat, then scraping the sweat off into a jar. If they want their arrows to kill, they dip the tips in the poison jar.

▲ Toucan
*The toucan uses its big beak to fight rival males and to eat fruit and birds' eggs. But no one knows just why it is so colorful.*

◄ Poisonous frog
*Some tree frogs like the kokoi and the poison-arrow have a poison much more deadly than any snake. Their bright colors act as a warning.*

▲ **Three-toed sloth**
*Sloths live in the jungles of South America. They live in trees, climbing and hanging upside down, using their long claws as hooks.*

### What bird has a beak as big as its body?

The toco toucan has a huge, brightly colored beak 9 inches (23cm) long—longer than its body. It doesn't overbalance because the beak is full of holes inside and so is very lightweight.

### What snakes squeeze victims to death?

"Constrictor" snakes like pythons wrap their coils around a victim and squeeze until they suffocate.

### What is the slowest creature in the jungle?

Hanging upside down in the trees, the three-toed tree sloth takes a minute to lope just 10 feet (3m). On the ground, it can manage only 6 feet (1.8m).

### What's the noisiest creature in the Amazon jungle?

Howler monkeys have a sound box in their throats that resonates very loudly. When a small group howls together, the noise can be heard over 2 miles (3km) away.

### What's a prehensile tail?

Monkeys in the New World—the Americas—often have prehensile tails. Monkeys in the Old World—Asia and Africa—don't. They are muscular tails that can curl to grip things like a hand, which is very useful for swinging through trees.

### What's a jaguar?

A jaguar is the biggest cat in the Americas. It looks like a leopard, but it is larger and has a shorter tail. Its spot pattern is also slightly different.

▼ **The reticulated python**
*This python, which lives in the forests of Asia, grows up to 33 feet (10m) long, and can swallow a goat whole—then not eat for a month.*

# QUIZ

1  The sloth moves so slowly that plants grow on it: true or false?

2  What is the world's smallest bird?

3  What is the world's loudest bird a) the great bittern b) the golden eagle c) the Indian peacock?

4  How much poison from the kokoi frog's sweat does it take to kill a man: a) 1 fluid oz. (27ml) b) 1 pint (450ml) c) 0.00001 oz. (0.0003 gm)

5  Cockatoos have been heard talking to each other in English: true or false?

6  Victorians used blue morpho butterflies as broaches: true or false?

**Answers**
1. True; algae grows in its fur, making it look green  2. The bee hummingbird is just 2.1 inches (57mm) long  3. c)  4. c)  5. False; they can mimic a few words but not converse  6. True

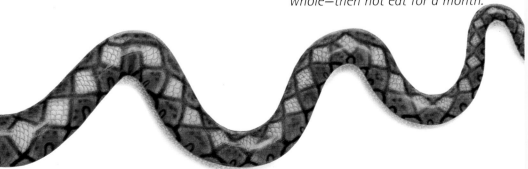

# Woodland animals

## What creatures live in woods?

MANY DIFFERENT ANIMALS live in woodlands in the temperate zone, in between the tropics and the poles. The leaf litter beneath the trees teems with tiny creatures-worms, millipedes, ants, and other insects-all of which draw predators such as spiders, shrews, and mice. The trees themselves provide a haven for many insects, birds, and small mammals.

### Why does a woodpecker peck wood ?

A woodpecker clings to tree trunks, propped up by its stiff tail, and rapidly hammers its long, powerful beak against the trunk. The idea is to bore a hole for nesting or to get at insects and grubs, which the woodpecker licks out with its long, wormlike tongue. The tip of the tongue is barbed so that the bird can harpoon tiny insects deep inside narrow tunnels.

### Where do badgers live?

Badgers live in families in extensive burrows called setts, which they dig out with their broad, powerful forepaws. American badgers live in the dry scrub of southwestern states. The smaller European badgers have their setts in woodlands, but they may also be in fields or even dumps.

### What do foxes eat?

Foxes eat all kinds of food. They often hunt at night for small animals such as voles and rabbits. But they also eat beetles, worms and berries. They are scavengers too, and in recent years, foxes have been seen in towns going through trashcans for scraps. Occasionally, when food is scarce they kill farmers' chickens.

### Why are foxes cunning?

Foxes are intelligent hunters with very keen senses of smell, sight, and hearing. These senses warn foxes about threats, helping them to escape from attackers. Farmers whose chickens have been stolen are the first to call them cunning as they cleverly elude capture.

◄ Red fox
*The fox is rather like a small dog, but the red fox, with its russet coat, large ears, bright amber eyes, and big, bushy tail, is unmistakable.*

▶ **Fallow deer**
*Herds of wild fallow deer have lived for centuries in the English royal forests such as the New Forest, where only the king and his courtiers could hunt them.*

## What are antlers?

Antlers are the hard, spiky branches of bone on a deer's head. They are used as weapons like horns, but antlers are different from horns and only male deer have them. Horns are permanent bony growths covered in horn, but antlers are covered in a hairy skin called velvet, and grow then drop off once a year.

## What are the smallest woodland carnivores?

Weasels, mink and wolverines are very fierce, despite their small size, and are able to kill animals such as rabbits that are much larger.

## What happens in the woods at night?

Many small mammals, such as shrews, moles, squirrels, mice, weasels, stoats, ferrets, and foxes, go hunting. So too do night-flying birds such as the nightjar, which sleeps camouflaged on the ground by day. And so does the tawny owl, which preys on the small mammals.

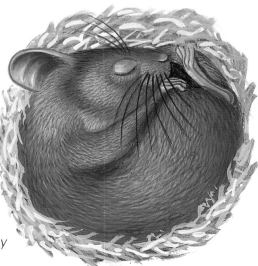

▶ **Wood mouse**
*Like many woodland mammals, wood mice go into a sleepy stage, almost like hibernation, in winter. This helps them save energy when food is scarce.*

# QUIZ

1  What is a female fox called?

2  What is the biggest woodland creature?

3  Do chipmunks build nests in trees?

4  What is the special long winter sleep of animals called?

5  What animal leaves tracks in the snow seeming to come down from a tree?

6  What is the smallest woodland mammal?

7  What is a female deer called?

8  An opossum is what type of mammal?

9  What is the wood mouse's most deadly enemy?

**Answers**
1. Vixen  2. Red deer  3. No—under twigs and stones  4. Hibernation  5. Squirrel  6. Pygmy shrew  7. Doe  8. Marsupial  9. Weasel

# Cold forest animals

## What animals live in cold forests?

THE FOREST TREES OF THE COLD NORTH are mainly conifers like pines and many of the woodland creatures feed on pine leaves and cones, including chipmunks, crossbills, and insects such as pine-shoot moths, and animals that prey on them, such as pine martens, owls, wolves, and bears.

### What do bears eat?

Brown bears eat almost anything. Fruits and berries, honey straight from bees' nests, fish, and carrion (carcasses left by other animals). They also hunt small mammals. They can even catch fish by scooping them out of the river with their paw. The technical name for such wide-ranging eaters is omnivore.

### Do bears hug?

The idea that bears hug their victims to death is an old wives' tale. They usually kill any animals they hunt with a swift blow or "cuff" from their huge, strong forepaws—or with a bite from their sharp teeth.

◀ **Big and brown**
*Bears usually move around on all fours. But they can often stand up to reach berries in trees. A standing male brown bear is a full seven feet tall—quite a bit taller than a man.*

▲ **Raccoon**
*Raccoons live near water because they often feed on frogs, crabs, water snails, and small fish.*

### What is the woodland bandit?

The raccoon of the forests of North America looks like a bandit because of the distinctive black eye mask across its white face. Equally distinctive is its big, bushy black and white striped tale.

### Do pine martens live in pines?

Pine martens are small creatures like weasels. They don't actually live in pine trees, but they are incredibly agile climbers—one of the few predators that can catch a squirrel in a tree.

## What's a moose yard?

In deep snow, a moose can easily be overcome by a marauding puma. So when herds of moose get together in winter, they trample out big flat areas of snow called "yards." Here they can get a good enough footing to give them a fighting chance of using their antlers and hooves on an attacker.

## Why does a beaver slap it's tail on the water?

To warn other beavers of approaching danger.

## Do reindeer pull sleighs?

Reindeer are one of the longest domesticated of all creatures. The people of Siberia were using them to pull sleighs and for riding more than 7,000 years ago.

◄ **The winter trek**
*In winter, when the weather in the cold north gets bitter and forage gets poor, reindeer begin a long trek to the south. In the past, they used to migrate in herds a quarter of a million strong.*

▶ **Big feller**
*Beavers can bring down literally scores of small trees to build dams and their homes on the river, gnawing through them with their two razor-sharp front teeth.*

# QUIZ

1  What do they call a pine marten in Russia?

2  What's the difference between a reindeer and a caribou?

3  What's a beaver's home called?

4  Which animal has the biggest horns?

5  Why's a grizzly bear grizzly?

6  What's the difference between a moose and an elk?

7  What is a lynx?

8  Does a wolf really howl at the moon?

**Answers**
1. A sable   2. None; a caribou is the North American name for a reindeer   3. A lodge   4. A moose   5. It has grey hairs among the black   6. None; moose is the North American name for an elk   7. A small wild cat   8. No, but they do howl at night to communicate with the rest of the pack.

43

# Animals of cold seas

**Big bird**
*The albatross is the world's largest seabird, more than 10 feet (3m) from wingtip to wingtip.*

## What animals live in the Arctic?

THE WEATHER GETS SO BITTERLY COLD in the Arctic that it is hard to imagine how any creatures can live there, yet a surprising number do–in the sea, including seals and whales; in the air, such as the Arctic tern; and on land, such as the polar bear, the Arctic fox, and the Arctic hare.

### Which bird never sees the sunset?

The Arctic tern lives in the Arctic only during the summer when the sun never completely sets. At the end of the summer, it makes an incredible 12,000-mile (20,000-km) flight to the other end of the world to catch the summer in Antarctica, where it remains daylight for months on end too.

### Are seals fish or mammals?

Despite their streamlined, fishlike shape, seals are warm-blooded mammals. Just like other mammals, they have babies that feed on their mother's milk.

### How does the snowshoe hare get its name?

The snowshoe hare, which goes white as snow in winter, gets its name from its huge feet, which act like snowshoes when it bounds easily across the softest snow. Long hair grows between the toes, both to stop the toes sinking into the snow, and to keep the hare's feet warm.

### How do seals keep warm?

On land, mammals rely on the air trapped in thick fur to keep them warm, but this is no good in the water. Seals have only a thin layer of fur, but they have, instead, a layer of fatty blubber under their skins up to 4 inches (10cm) thick.

Harp seal

◄ **Ice birds**
*Penguins are Antarctica's most distinctive inhabitants. Penguins can't fly, and they waddle ungainly on land, but they are agile swimmers, using their wings as flippers.*

## How do Emperor penguins keep their eggs warm?

Emperor penguins are the only birds to lay their eggs in the bitter Antarctic winter. They keep them warm by resting them on their feet, tucked under their belly.

## Do all penguins live in the Antarctic?

All 18 species of penguin live in the southern hemisphere, and most live in or near Antarctica.

▼ **Seals and sea lions**
*Seals and sea lions are different. Only sea lions have external ears and also back flippers that they can use to move about on land.*

## What is the biggest creature of cold seas?

The Blue whale, the biggest creature in the world, which grows more than 100 feet (30m) long and weighs from 90 to 180 tons.

## How do whales communicate?

By clicks, whistles and low-pitch rumbles which echo hundreds of kilometres through the water. The humpback whale sings like this.

Sea lion

# QUIZ

1  What is the biggest penguin?

2  What bird makes the longest migration?

3  What sea mammals have two long tusks?

4  What color do Arctic foxes go in winter?

5  What do seals eat?

6  How many kinds of animals breed in the Antarctic:  a) 1 b) 8 c) 49?

7  What ox lives in the Arctic?

8  How do whales breathe out?

9  Which is the largest meat-eater in the Arctic?

**Answers**
1. Emperor penguin  2. Arctic Tern  3. Walrus  4. White
5. Mainly fish  6. b), four kinds of seal, two kinds of penguin, the southern skua, and the snow petrel  7. Musk ox
8. Through the blowhole on top of their heads  9. Polar bear

45

# African animals

## What animals live in Africa?

AFRICA IS HOME TO SOME of the world's most spectacular animals. The tropical forest in the center is home to many different kinds of monkeys as well as apes such as the gorilla. In the bush country or savanna beyond live such magnificent creatures as elephants, lions, giraffes, rhinos, hippos, zebras, and many more.

▲ **Amboseli, Kenya**
*Many of Africa's most spectacular animals have been reduced almost to extinction by hunters who call them "Big Game." Now many animals are protected inside safari parks such as the Amboseli in the shadow of Mount Kilimanjaro.*

## How do lions hunt?

Although they sometimes attack young giraffes or weak buffaloes, lions' main prey is antelopes. Lions hunt silently, usually in small groups—lying in wait for the antelopes at waterholes or creeping stealthily through the grass. When they near their prey, they make a sudden sprint, then pounce, sinking their sharp fangs into their victim's neck. Meat is so nutritious that one kill is usually enough to last a lion for days.

## Why do elephants have trunks?

An elephant uses its trunk for all kinds of different tasks. The trunk is used mainly for feeding and the elephant pulls off grasses and leaves with it and stuffs them in its mouth. But the elephant also uses the trunk to suck up water, which it then drinks or uses to spray itself clean. The trunk is the elephant's nose too, and an elephant may often put its trunk in the air to sniff the wind. The trunk is even used for caressing baby elephants.

## How can you tell an African elephant from an Asian elephant?

African elephants are generally bigger than Asian elephants. African elephants have much bigger ears and much longer tusks. The Asian elephant also has a slightly humped back and just one fingerlike lip on the end of its trunk, while the African has two. The African elephant lives on hot, dry plains, while the Asian lives in shady forests.

▶ **Big bird**
*Africa is home not only to the largest land mammal, the elephant, but the largest bird too—the ostrich. Ostriches can reach 8 feet (2.5m) tall. They can't fly, but they can run fast, and their long legs can inflict a hefty kick.*

◀ **Deadly huntress**
*Male lions with their big manes may look impressive, but it is the females, called lionesses, that do most of the hunting.*

## How tall is a giraffe?
A male giraffe can grow up to 18 feet (5.5m) tall, taller than any other animal. Its legs are long, and its neck is even longer. With such a long neck a giraffe can feed on leaves high in the trees that other animals can't reach.

## How does a giraffe drink?
Its long legs and neck mean a giraffe has a long way to bend for a drink. So it has to either spread its front legs very wide or kneel right down—making it vulnerable to attack by lions.

◄ **Tall order**
*Giraffes reach high branches with their long necks, but the leaves they eat aren't soft and succulent. Giraffes eat branches of thorn trees—prickles and all.*

## Can hippos swim?
A hippo spends most of its day in or near water, only coming out at night to feed on plants. Yet it cannot really swim. Instead it walks or runs along the riverbed, often at amazing speeds, only coming up for air occasionally.

## What is a gnu?
A gnu or wildebeest is a large African antelope that migrates across the plains between waterholes in huge herds.

## Why do zebras have stripes?
Zebras' stripes seem hard to miss. But in the shimmering heat of Africa, they act as camouflage, blurring the zebra's outline, like shadows of grass, especially when the zebra is moving slowly.

## How many kinds of zebra are there?
Three: the common, the mountain, and Grevy's zebra. The Grevy is the biggest, and brays like an ass.

# QUIZ

1  What's the world's fastest runner?
2  How fast can an ostrich fly?
3  What's a group of lions called?
4  What's the world's biggest mammal?
5  What animal has a horn on the end of its snout?
6  How can you tell a male lion from a female?
7  What's an okapi?
8  What are elephant's tusks made of?
9  Do zebras neigh like horses?

**Answers**
1. The cheetah, reaching speeds of up to 66 mph (110kp/h)
2. An ostrich can't fly at all
3. A pride 4. The Blue whale
5. A rhinoceros 6. An adult male has a big mane; a lioness has not
7. A relative of the giraffe
8. Ivory 9. No, they bark or bray.

# Wetland animals

▲ Cool crocodile
*Crocodiles adjust their lives to the weather, basking on the bank to warm up, but slipping into the water when it gets too hot.*

## What animals live in wetlands?

**W**ETLANDS ARE AMONG THE WORLD'S most precious animal habitats, havens for many wild creatures. Not only are there big animals like crocodiles and alligators, but smaller creatures like coypus and voles, and numerous birds, insects and, of course, fish.

## What's the difference between a crocodile and an alligator?

Alligators are generally rounder and fatter, with short, blunt snouts. Crocodiles are slightly thinner, and their snouts are longer and thinner. Crocodiles also have a fourth tooth on the lower jaw that can be seen when their mouths are shut.

## Are crocodiles like dinosaurs?

Crocodiles may be the nearest thing to dinosaurs alive today. Many dinosaurs may have had the same scaly skin and creatures very like crocodiles lived in the early Triassic Period, 200 million years ago, when the dinosaurs first appeared. But dinosaur's legs were underneath, not sticking out to the side like a crocodile's. Some people believe that dinosaurs' nearest living relatives are birds.

## Are there any other creatures like crocodiles?

Crocodiles belong to a group of animals called the crocodilians. Besides various species of crocodiles and alligators, the group includes smaller crocodile-like animals called caimans and gharials. Caimans have bony plates on their bellies. The gharial has a distinctive long, thin snout.

## Why is a flamingo pink?

For a long while, flamingos in zoos kept losing their delicate pink color and fading to white. Then keepers realized the problem was due to their diet. Flamingos feed on a certain kind of algae and these algae contain chemicals called cartenoids that are responsible for the pink. If a flamingo does not get these algae, it does not get the cartenoids, and its color fades.

▼ Wetland hunter
*Crocodiles live in the rivers and swamps of the tropics. They are fearsome hunters, with massive, snapping jaws—yet it is their tail that is most lethal. Crocodiles lie in wait in the shallows, looking for all the world like a log, until animals come to drink at the water. Then they make a sudden lunge at their victim, drag it into the water, and stun it with a blow from its tail, and drown it.*

The eyes and nostrils stick out of the water even when the crocodile is submerged

A crocodile's teeth do not overlap when the jaw is closed, unlike an alligator's

◀ **Spoon bill**

*A spoonbill is a large wading bird that paddles through swamps in the tropics dragging its long spoon-shaped bill through the water from side to side. It is searching for shrimps and other small water creatures and when it finds a meal, it snaps the bill shut on its victim like a pair of spring-loaded sugar tongs.*

## What's special about Okavango?

The Okavango Delta in Botswana is one of the world's largest wetlands, swelling to 8,500 square miles (22,000 sq km) in the wet season. A continual outflow and inflow of water keeps the water fresh and turns it into an astonishingly rich habitat—home to hippos, crocodiles, and elephants, as well as antelopes and countless birds and fish. But the Delta is coming under increasing threat from human activities.

The crocodile's tail is immensely powerful

Many crocodiles have been killed for their shiny, scaly skin

# QUIZ

1 **What's so remarkable about the mudskipper?**

2 **What gives the proboscis monkey of Borneo its name?**

3 **Where would you find a terrapin?**

4 **What is the Everglade kite?**

5 **Is it true that a mother crocodile carries her babies between her teeth?**

6 **Can crocodiles climb trees?**

7 **Are leeches good for you?**

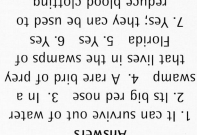

**Answers**
1. It can survive out of water  2. Its big red nose  3. In a swamp  4. A rare bird of prey that lives in the swamps of Florida  5. Yes  6. Yes  7. Yes; they can be used to reduce blood clotting

# Mountain animals

## What animals live on mountains?

COLD AND WINDY, mountaintops are among the harshest environments in the world, but surprisingly many animals can survive here, including hunting animals such as pumas and snow leopards as well as sure-footed grazers, such as mountain goats, chamois, ibex, and yaks.

▲ **Lammergeier**
*The huge lammergeier is one of the few birds that can survive in the high mountain peaks. They are superb gliders, floating over the slopes looking for carcasses for hours, seemingly without effort.*

▼ **Himalayan Snowcock**
*The Himalayan Snowcock is one of the highest living of all birds, nesting more than 13,000 feet (3,900m) up in the Himalayan mountains. Its gray and white plumage blends perfectly with the landscape of gray rock and snow.*

### Why does the lammergeier drop its dinner?

The lammergeier is a kind of vulture found in Africa and southern Europe. Food is scarce in the mountains, so the lammergeier has learned to feed on the toughest hide and bones in a carcass, too tough for other animals. But some bones are too tough even for the lammergeier. So it drops the bones again and again from a great height on to its own chosen rock (called an ossuary)—until the bone smashes and the bird can get at the soft marrow inside.

### What is the world's biggest bird of prey?

The condors of California and the South American Andes are the world's biggest birds of prey with huge wings more than 10 feet (3m) across. They are actually vultures, feeding on carcasses, and soaring for hours on the buffeting winds that howl through the peaks while they wait for an animal to die.

▲ **Yak pack**
*In Tibet, the docile yak has been domesticated and is used as a pack animal, as well as for milk and meat, and for its wooly coat.*

### What is highest living mammal?

The yak is a remarkable ox with huge curved horns and a very shaggy coat that lives in the Himalayan mountains of Tibet, the world's highest mountains. Protected from the cold by its coat and able to eat the toughest grass, it can survive over 20,000 feet (6,000m) up among the peaks.

▶ **Snow cat**

*The snow leopard is a big cat that lives in the Himalayan mountains. It has a beautiful pale coat with dark markings, which has sadly made it a target for fur poachers.*

## How do mountain goats climb?

Mountain goats are incredibly nimble climbers, able to get up the steepest slopes and leap from crag to crag with amazing agility. Their secret lies not only in their sense of balance but in their hooves. A mountain goat's hooves have sharp edges which dig into rock crevices. They also have slightly hollow soles, which act almost like suction pads.

## What is a chamois?

A chamois is a tiny animal that leaps around the highest peaks in Europe. It is a kind of goat-antelope, with the face and horns of an antelope and the mountaineering abilities (and smell) of a goat.

## What dogs live in mountains?

The timber wolf looks rather like a German shepherd dog. It has been driven from lowland forests in North America, but many still survive high in the mountains, hunting their prey in packs.

## What animal can jump highest?

The puma, also known as the cougar or mountain lion, can jump an astonishing 18 feet (5.5m) into the air to get into a tree or jump up on a ledge. This is the equivalent of jumping up to an upstairs bedroom window—and much higher than any kangaroo, which can only jump 10 feet (3m).

## What was the highest climbing cat?

In September 1950, a four-month old kitten belonging to a little Swiss girl named Josephine Aufdenblatten began following a group of climbers. It followed them all the way to the top of the famous Alpine peak, the 14,688-foot (4,478-m) high Matterhorn!

## What happens in winter to a mountain hare's coat?

Like the coat of many animals in snowy places, the mountain hare's coat, or "pelage," turns white so that it is much harder for predators to spot against the white of the snow.

# Desert animals

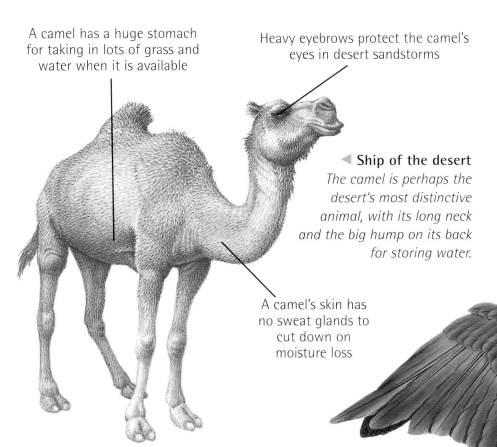

## Do animals live in the desert?

**D**ESERTS ARE HARD PLACES FOR ANIMALS to live. They are very dry and often very hot too. Many insects, spiders and scorpions, as well as lizards and snakes have adapted to life under these harsh conditions, but mammals such as the camel survive here too.

▲ **Sand cat**
*The desert even has its own predatory cat—the sand cat. It is quite small, and by hunting only at night, it can survive in hot deserts.*

### How do kangaroo rats save water?

The kangaroo rat gets its name from its big hind legs. It can survive even in California's Death Valley because it gets its water from fats in its food and saves water by eating its own droppings.

### What antelope lives in the desert?

The Sahara desert has its own large antelope, the addax. It never needs a waterhole, because it gets all its water from its food.

### How do camels cope with the desert sand?

Camel's feet have just two joined toes to stop their feet sinking into soft sand or snow, in the case of the Bactrian camel of central Asia. They also have nostril's that close up completely to block out the sand, and double rows of eyelashes to protect their eyes from both sand and the sun's glare.

A camel has a huge stomach for taking in lots of grass and water when it is available

Heavy eyebrows protect the camel's eyes in desert sandstorms

◄ **Ship of the desert**
*The camel is perhaps the desert's most distinctive animal, with its long neck and the big hump on its back for storing water.*

A camel's skin has no sweat glands to cut down on moisture loss

### What does a camel have a hump for?

The camel's hump is made of fat, not water as some people insist. But the fat can be broken down within the body and converted to both energy and water, whenever food and water is scarce.

▶ **Bearded vultures**
*Vultures gather to feed around the carcasses of dead animals. Here the vultures are bearded vultures which get their name from the clump of black bristles under their beaks; the carcass is an antelope.*

Desert hedgehog

Fennec fox

Jerboa

▲ The burrowers

*A number of small animals cope with the desert heat by resting in burrows or sheltering under stones in the day, and only coming out to feed in the cool of the night. The fennec fox also has big ears to help it keep cool by radiating heat.*

## Do birds live in the desert?

Although many birds, like vultures, live in fairly dry parts of the world, only a few live in true deserts. Among these is the sand grouse. It rests under bushes during the day, then flies hundreds of miles at night to watering places. It soaks up water in breast feathers to help protect its young from the sun.

## Do vultures hunt?

No. Vultures are mainly scavengers, which means they feed on animals that have died already, or been killed by other animals such as lions. Their strong claws and beaks are for tearing carcasses apart. Each species feeds on a different bit of the carcass. So small Egyptian vultures wait until big lappet-faced vultures have finished before diving in.

# QUIZ

1  What is a gila monster?

2  How many humps does a camel have?

3  What is a dromedary?

4  Where is a scorpion's sting?

5  How do lizards survive the desert heat?

6  What is the biggest desert in the world?

7  What continent does the kangaroo rat live on?

8  What is the biggest animal in the desert?

**Answers**
1. A Mexican desert lizard with a poisonous bite  2. The Asian or Bactrian has two; the Arabian, one.  3. An Arabian camel for racing  4. The tip of its tail  5. By sheltering under rocks during the hottest part of the day  6. The Sahara  7. North America  8. The camel

# Seashore life

## What makes the seashore special?

**W**ATER IS CONTINUALLY moving up and down the seashore as waves roll up and down, and as the tide rises and falls. So creatures that live on the seashore have to be well adapted to surviving long periods out of water–or long periods in salt water. The seashore, then, has its own special creatures, including crabs, anemones, and a range of shellfish such as barnacles and limpets.

Common gull

▼ Rock pool
*Rock pools are seashore aquariums full of all kinds of sea life.*
**Key**:
1. *Mussels*
2. *Starfish*
3. *Cladophora*
4. *Gem anemone*
5. *Common prawn*
6. *Bladder wrack*
7. *Common goby*
8. *Dog whelk*
9. *Barnacles*
10. *Sugar weed*
11. *Cockle*
12. *Limpet*

▶ Crab
*Crabs have a hard shell, eight legs, and two powerful pincers for grabbing prey. They scuttle along the beach or the seabed sideways.*

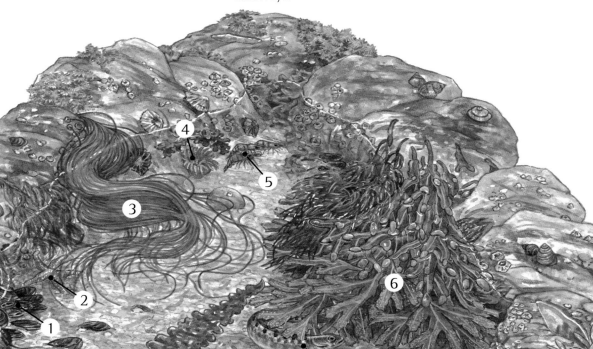

## ▶ Puffin and guillemot

*A huge number of birds live by the sea, feeding on the seashore or diving for fish in the sea. Most have webbed feet for swimming, waterproof plumage and sharp bills for gripping fish. The puffin's big colourful beak can hold up to 11 fish at once. Puffins live in burrows on clifftops. Guillemots nest in big, closely-packed colonies on narrow cliff ledges.*

Guillemot

Puffin

## What lives in rock pools?

Rock pools are pools of seawater left behind on seashore rocks as the tide goes out. They can get so warm and salty in the sunshine that they have their own special range of creatures, including shrimps, hermit crabs, fish such as blennies and gobies, anemones, and sea slugs.

## What creature looks like a blob of jelly?

The beadlet anemone looks just like a blob of purple jelly stuck on the rocks when half uncovered by the tide. But when they are completely submerged, they open to reveal a ring of tentacles which they use to trap the small creatures they feed on. They look a bit like flowers, which is how they get their name, but even though they never move, they are in fact carnivorous animals.

## What is a mollusk?

Mollusks are a huge group of creatures including slugs and snails, clams and oysters, octopuses and squids that live mostly in water or damp places. They are mostly soft, squidgy creatures, but octopuses and squids are protected by stinging tentacles and shellfish and snails by shells.

## What creatures live on beaches?

Sandy shores often look completely lifeless, but just below the surface are often all kinds of creatures burrowing in the sand to escape from the drying wind and sun, and also from hungry predators. They include razor clams, lugworms, sea cucumbers, small crabs, and burrowing sea anemones. Some filter food from seawater; others eat tiny particles from the sand. Along the hightide line you might see sandhoppers which look like tiny yellow woodlice, feeding on rotting seaweed.

# QUIZ

1 Puffins talk to each other by growling: true or false?

2 What does a sea urchin use its spikes for?

3 How many legs do barnacles have?

4 Why do fiddler crabs waggle their pincers a) to attract a mate b) to swim c) to frighten prey?

5 What color are lobsters?

6 The sooty tern can fly nonstop for 10 years: true or false?

7 Kittiwakes get their name because they dive toward sleeping cats: true or false?

8 The common gull feeds on dumps in big cities: true or false?

Answers
1. True 2. Walking 3. 10 4. a) 5. Blue; they only go red when cooked 6. True 7. False 8. True

12

# Australian animals

▲ **Dingo**
*The dingo is Australia's own wild dog, the only large carnivore. But it is a scavenger, not a hunter.*

▲ **Wombat**
*Wombats look a little like bears, but they behave more like rabbits, living in burrows and feeding on bark, roots, and grass.*

▶ **Kangaroo**
*The kangaroo is the biggest of the marsupials. But a newborn kangaroo is smaller than a thumb—and blind and deaf—when it makes its amazing way up through its mother's fur from the birth opening, up through her belly fur and into the pouch.*

## What's strange about Australian animals?

AUSTRALIA HAS ANIMALS LIKE NOWHERE else in the world. The land links to Asia were cut off millions of years ago, and a unique set of pouched animals called marsupials developed, along with many other unusual creatures.

### What are marsupials?
Babies of ordinary mammals grow fully inside their mother before they're born. Marsupial babies grow only partially, and are born so tiny they can't survive in the open. After they're born, they crawl into a pouch on their mother's belly and stay there until they're big enough to climb out.

### Can marsupials fly?
No, but squirrel-like creatures called gliders come close. They have big flaps of skin stretched between their legs, so when they leap from tree to tree, they can glide long distances. The best flier is the great gliding possum.

### Is the koala a bear?
No. It looks just like a big teddy bear, but the koala is not related to any bear. It is a marsupial belonging to a group of animals called phalangers, which includes the possum. When born, a baby koala crawls into its mother's pouch. After six months, it climbs round on to her back and rides piggyback.

### What bird sounds like a chainsaw?
The male lyre bird is one of the world's weirdest sounding birds. To attract a female, it imitates any sound it hears—including machines. It mimics a chainsaw starting up and hacking through wood, for instance, so well that people are fooled into thinking they're hearing the real thing.

### What's a Tasmanian devil?
A fierce little marsupial that lives in Tasmania and looks like a cross between a black rat and a dog. It eats rats, wallabies, and birds—not to mention sheep, chickens, and poisonous snakes.

▲ **Koala and baby**
*Koalas eat only the leaves and bark of certain eucalyptus, or "gum," trees. So they live only in a small area where these trees grow in eastern Australia.*

▼ **Marsupial mole**
*Many creatures in the rest of the world have their marsupial equivalent in Australia—even the humble mole.*

### How far can a 'roo jump?
Kangaroos' huge back legs help them jump huge distances. They can bound along at nearly 30 mph (50km/h), covering 30 feet (9m) or so at every single leap.

●

### What's a duck-billed platypus?
The duck–billed platypus is a mammal with four legs and fur — but with webbed feet and a beak like a duck's. What's more, it is a "monotreme" which means it is one of the few mammals that lays eggs.

# QUIZ

1  What is a baby kangaroo called?

2  What is a wallaby?

3  Is a wallaby bigger than a kangaroo?

4  What do bandicoots eat?

5  Is a cuscus: a) an Arabian meal b) a possum c) a very awkward man?

6  What does "playing possum" mean?

7  Is a quoll or dasyure a kind of: a) rat b) bat c) cat?

8  How does the kookaburra get its name?

9  What is a thorny devil and is it dangerous?

**Answers**
1. A Joey  2. A small kangaroo-like animal  3. No  4. Insect grubs  5. b)  6. Playing dead, as a possum does to escape predators  7. c)  8. From its rippling call  9. A harmless thorny lizard

# Freshwater animals

## What animals live close to rivers and lakes?

THE RIVERS AND LAKES of the world teem with all kinds of small creatures–small mammals such as voles, water rats, and otters, birds such as kingfishers and herons, insects such as dragonflies and water boatmen and, of course, many freshwater fish such as trout.

### Why do some birds have long thin legs?

Birds that have long thin legs are generally wading birds, such redshanks, avocets, and herons. They need their long legs for wading through the water to look for insects and worms. The biggest wading birds are herons, storks, and flamingoes.

### Why do ducks have bills?

Ducks have broad, flat bills because they feed on insects that live in the water. The broad bill enables them to scoop up a big gulp of water and filter out the insects. "Dabbling" ducks such as mallards and widgeons simply upend in shallow water. "Diving ducks" such as scoters dive to the bottom.

### How does a kingfisher catch fish?

By sitting on a perch above the water silently watching for fish. When it sees a minnow or a trout, the kingfisher dives into the water in a flash, then flies back to its perch, tosses the fish in the air and swallows it.

### Why do frogs have long legs?

To help them jump huge distances to escape predators. A small frog can jump several yards—the equivalent of a human jumping the length of a football field. Frogs also have strong front legs to withstand the shock of landing.

### What's a tadpole?

A tadpole is a young frog, soon after it emerges from its egg. A tadpole looks like a little black fish, but after seven weeks or so it will grow two back legs and get a frog face. After 10 weeks, its legs are quite long and it has front legs as well. By 12-14 weeks, the tail is gone, and it emerges from the water as a frog.

▲ Otter
*Otters live close to rivers and lakes in North America, Europe, and Asia. Their lithe, powerful bodies make them strong swimmers, and they can dive for five minutes at a time.*

▲ Barheaded goose
*Geese, ducks, and swans are all water fowl, with webbed feet and long, supple necks for reaching down into the water.*

◄ Common frog
*Frogs have two big swiveling eyes to help them judge distances when jumping and catching flies.*

## How do young otters spend their day?

Otters are mainly nocturnal animals, coming out of their dens in the riverbanks at night to hunt for fish in the river. But young otters are among the most playful of all animals, and they can often be seen during the day tumbling and rolling happily around on the bank, sliding down mud chutes, and leaping in and out of the water.

## What's a coypu?

A coypu is a large water rat, more than 3 feet (90cm) long and related to the guinea pig. It comes originally from South America, but was brought to North America and Europe by fur farmers and has thrived in rivers and marshes.

## Is a water vole a rat?

No, though people sometimes call them water rats. The vole prefers clean water, unlike the rat. The water vole is now becoming very rare, partly due to mink predation.

## Why don't fish sink?

Because they have a special air bag inside their bodies called a swim bladder. This acts like the air in a lifejacket, keeping the fish afloat. Without it, the fish would have to swim continuously

## Why don't fish drown?

Fish breathe through gills, not lungs. Gills are rows of feathery brushes under flaps on the fish's head. The fish gulps in water through its mouth,and lets it out through the gill covers. As the water passes over the feathery surfaces of the gill, they absorb oxygen from the water just as our lungs do from the air.

## What is the main predator in European rivers?

The pike can grow to over 65 pounds (30kg). Long and sleek, with a large mouth full of sharp teeth, the pike is a deadly hunter that lurks among the weeds waiting for fish, or even rats and birds, waiting to pounce. This is why it prefers deep ponds and slow rivers.

◁ **Fish**
*Bream is a common freshwater fish that was once the staple diet of poor people in Europe. Rainbow trout is a native of North American rivers and fast-flowing streams.*

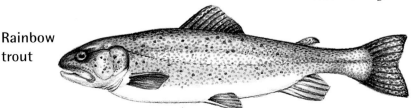

**Bream**

**Rainbow trout**

# QUIZ

1  Do water voles eat any meat?

2  What bird is famous for its boom?

3  What is a water boatman?

4  What is an amphibian?

5  What is a young eel called?

6  What is the real name for an otter's den ?

7  What fish leaps up waterfalls?

8  What is a young dragonfly called?

9  How many legs does a crayfish have?

10 What is the jelly called frog spawn?

# Grassland animals

## What animals live on grasslands?

SOME GRASSLANDS ARE HOT. Some are quite cool. But they are all home to large herds of grazing animals such as antelopes, buffalo, and horses, and the animals that prey upon them, such as big cats like lions and cheetahs.

Wildebeest

### Why do antelopes have long legs?

There is nowhere for a large animal to hide in open grasslands, so nearly all grassland animals are fast runners with long legs.

### How fast can an antelope run?

Cheetahs can reach 66 mph (110km/h) when chasing antelopes, but only for a short distance. The pronghorn antelope has been timed at 41 mph (67km/h) for well over 10 miles (16km) but has a top speed of more than 60 mph (98km/h).

### Are all antelope horns the same?

There are more than 60 species of antelope living in Africa and southern Asia—and each has different-shaped horns.

▲ **Grazing herds**

*Grasslands in the tropics are the home of vast herds of antelopes of various kinds. In the last century, herds of 10 million springboks, hundreds of miles long, were sometimes seen in South Africa.*

▲ **Cheetah**

*The fastest runner in the world, the cheetah shows an astonishing turn of speed over a short distance to catch gazelles—a kind of antelope.*

### Which is the biggest antelope?

The biggest antelope is the giant eland of Africa, which has now become very rare. It stands over 6 feet (1.8m) tall at the shoulder, and weighs about a ton. The smallest is the royal antelope, which is very tiny—no bigger than a hare.

### What's odd about cheetahs?

Cheetahs are not like other big cats. In fact, some scientists think they are not that closely related. They have a much longer, flatter head than other cats. They also have permanently extended claws on the end of very long legs.

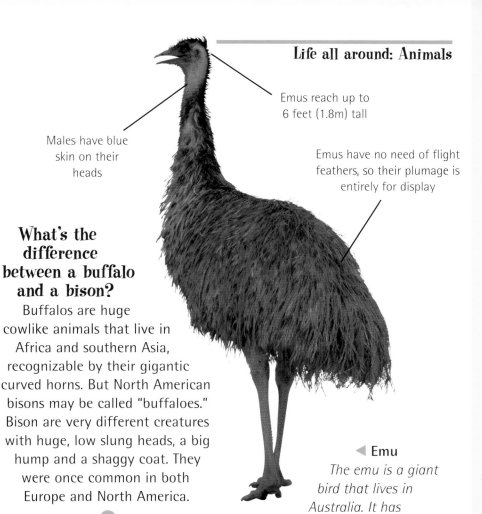

Emus reach up to 6 feet (1.8m) tall

Emus have no need of flight feathers, so their plumage is entirely for display

Males have blue skin on their heads

## What's the difference between a buffalo and a bison?

Buffalos are huge cowlike animals that live in Africa and southern Asia, recognizable by their gigantic curved horns. But North American bisons may be called "buffaloes." Bison are very different creatures with huge, low slung heads, a big hump and a shaggy coat. They were once common in both Europe and North America.

## Do horses have toes?

Yes. All the big grazing animals have toes, even hooved animals. They are divided in two big groups. Ungulates, including horses, rhinos, and tapirs, have an even number of toes on each foot. Artiodactyls, such as pigs, cows, and camels, have an odd number of toes.

## What are the world's biggest birds?

The world's biggest birds are all flightless birds, including the ostrich and the cassowary, with very long legs for running and long necks. The biggest, the North African ostrich, lives on the fringes of the Sahara desert and grows up to 9 feet (2.7m) tall.

◀ **Emu**
*The emu is a giant bird that lives in Australia. It has virtually no wings and can't fly but, like ostriches and cassowaries, it can run very fast on its long, powerful legs. Emus are rather inquisitive birds. They feed on fruit and insects but may often steal coins and keys.*

## What was the biggest bird ever?

Bones found in New Zealand show that until 1,000 years ago, there was a bird called the moa, which was as tall as an elephant. When the first bone was found in 1839 some people thought that it did indeed belong to an elephant. It was the eminent Victorian naturalist Richard Owen who worked out what the bone really belonged to.

# QUIZ

1  How do cows 'chew the cud'?
2  What is an animal that eats plants called?
3  What animal has the longest horns of all?
4  How fast can an ostrich run:
   a) 12 mph (20km/h)
   b) 24 mph (40km/h)
   c) 36 mph (60km/h)?
5  What is an oryx?
6  What are prairie dogs?
7. Is it true that prairie dogs kiss each other when they meet?
8. How does a springbok get its name?
9. Were horses' ancestors bigger or smaller?

Answers
1. By rechewing partially digested food  2. A herbivore  3. Buffaloes  4. c)  5. A kind of antelope  6. A large, hamster-like creature that lives in big burrows beneath the prairies  7. Yes  8. By springing up to 10 feet (3m) straight up  9. Smaller

# Deep sea animals

## What creatures live in the sea?

LIFE BEGAN IN THE OCEANS and now a huge range of creatures live there. There are thousands of kinds of fish, from tiny gobies to giant whale sharks. There are also many shellfish, including mollusks such as clams and squids, and crustaceans such as shrimp and lobsters—not mention echinoderms such as sea urchins and sea cucumbers. Then there are various reptiles like sea snakes, amphibians such as turtles, and even a few a mammals such as seals and whales.

▼ **The great white shark**
*Sharks have powerful jaws and double rows of razor sharp teeth. When the outer row wears out or breaks, the inner row moves forward to replace them.*

### How big are whales?
Most full-grown whales are quite big, but the biggest of all—the Blue whale—is absolutely gigantic. It is the largest creature that has ever lived. An average Blue whale is over 100 feet (30m) and weighs some 90 tons. Some can grow twice as heavy. The biggest ever caught weighed 190 tons.

### Are dolphins and whales related?
Yes. Dolphins are a kind of whale. In fact, the biggest of the 37 kinds of dolphin is called the killer whale. Together, whales, dolphins, and porpoises are known as cetaceans.

▲ Giant turtle
*The leatherback, the world's biggest turtle, grows 10 feet (3m) long and can weigh 2.5 tons.*

### What is the fiercest shark?
The great white shark is one of the biggest and most fearsome of the sharks. Attacks by sharks on humans are quite rare, but most of the time it is great whites that are the culprits. They live all around the world in warm waters, and can grow up to 23 feet (7m) long. Their double rows of razor-sharp teeth can rip through sheet steel.

▶ **Different levels in the sea**

*Different creatures live at
different levels in the sea.*

1. *Dolphin*
2. *Jellyfish*
3. *Plant plankton*
4. *Zoo (animal) plankton*
5. *Tuna*
6. *Turtle*
7. *Whale*
8. *Squid*
9. *Deep sea fish, including
angler fish and gulper eel.*

## How do fish stay afloat?

Fish stay afloat because they have a special air bag inside their bodies called a swim bladder. Without this, they would have to swim all the time. As a fish swims deeper, the extra pressure of water squeezes more gas made in the blood into the bladder. As the fish swims up again, this extra gas is let out, so the fish floats easily.

## Are any fish poisonous?

Quite a few, such as the pufferfish. The most poisonous is the stonefish, whose fins have spines containing a deadly neurotoxin, which can kill in minutes.

## How do fish breath underwater?

Fish get oxygen from the water just as we get oxygen from the air. But they absorb the oxygen through gills, which are feathery brushes under flaps on the side of the fish's head. To take oxygen in, the fish gulps water through its mouth, swashes it over the gills and lets it out through the gill flaps.

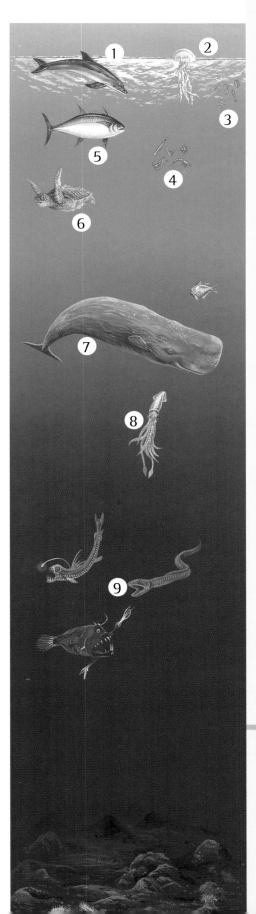

# QUIZ

1  What shark has a head shaped like a mallet?

2  Some fish can fly 500 yards (450m) over the water; true or false?

3  What fish has a long lancelike nose?

4  Some fish can survive many days out of water: true of false?

5  The catfish makes a noise like a bagpipe with its swim bladder: true or false

6  Parrot fish get their name because they eat nuts like parrots: true or false?

7  What whale is famous for its singing?

8  What fish can blow itself up to three times its normal size?

**Answers**
1. The hammerhead shark
2. True, flying fish can
3. Swordfish  4. True  5. True
6. False  7. The humpback whale  8. The pufferfish

What was the
Stone Age?

Who were the
first farmers?

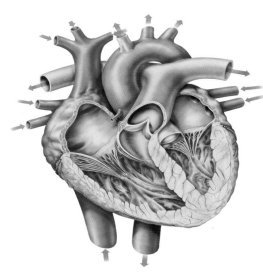

Who built the first
roof gardens?

Who first wore
trousers?

Why does vomit
taste sour?

What food makes
you grow?

How long are your
guts?

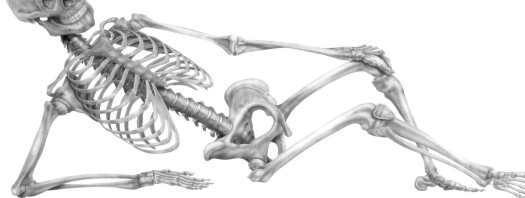

Why is blood red?

What's a brain?

How do you smell?

# People

Why do ears pop?

How many muscles has a football player?

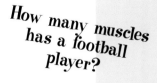

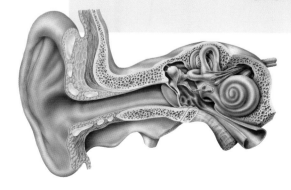

Why do we have two eyes?

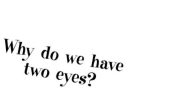

# Human origins

## When did the first humans live?

THE FIRST TRUE HUMANS lived about 30,000 years ago, but there were humanlike creatures millions of years earlier. Scientists call these humanlike creatures hominids, and there were many different kinds. The earliest hominids were very like apes, with long arms and a big jaw, but over time they evolved (changed) to become more and more like humans. Hominids and apes probably had the same ancestor–an orangutan-like creature that lived in Africa six million years ago.

▲ Cave painting of a horse
*Both Neanderthal Man and early humans often lived in caves and left behind extraordinary paintings on the wall—mainly of the animals they hunted.*

### Who were the first hominids?

Some of the oldest remains of hominids date from around four million years ago and belong to a group of creatures called Australopithecus. Australopithecus means "southern ape." Most southern apes walked upright like humans but were little more than 3 feet (90cm) tall. They had a smallish brain, jutting apelike jaws and hairy bodies, and lived on fruit and vegetables.

### Who first used tools?

Humans are not the only creatures to use tools. So do many animals such as sea otters. All early hominids probably did. But the first hominid to use tools with skill was *Homo habilis*, or "Handy Man," who appeared about two million years ago. Handy Man was the first really humanlike creature. He had a large brain and used tools to cut hides to make clothes and food for eating.

### Where did hominids live?

All early hominids lived in Africa, and only began to spread out further two million years ago. The first humans may have come from Africa too.

◄ Making fire
*Learning to make fire was one of Homo Erectus's greatest achievements. It not only kept him warm in winter, allowing him to live in cold places. It also meant he could cook food, and so eat meat.*

▲ Ancient home
*Early humans were usually nomadic and lived in tents made of hide, bones and sticks rather than permanent houses.*

Homo habilis
(Handy Man)

Australopithecus
(Southern Ape)

## Who were the first hunters?

The earliest hominids were vegetarians like apes. But about 1.5-2 million years ago, a kind of hominid called *Homo erectus*, or Upright Man, began to hunt and eat meat. Upright Man could light fires, cook food, and hunt with wooden spears. Upright Man was also the first hominid to spread out of Africa, and remains have been found as far away as Russia and Indonesia.

## Who was Neanderthal Man?

We humans belong to a group of creatures called *Homo sapiens*, or Wise Man, and Neanderthal Man was the first Wise Man, appearing about 100,000 years ago. He had a bigger brain than ours and a rugged body, and no one knows why he died out.

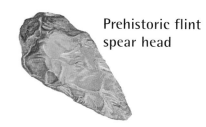

Prehistoric flint spear head

## What was the Stone Age?

Until humans discovered how to make tools from bronze about 6,000 years ago, humans made their tools from stone. So all of human history, from the time Upright Man appeared two million years ago until the beginning of the Bronze Age 6,000 years ago, is called the Stone Age. The Stone Age is divided into three periods: the Paleolithic or Old Stone Age from two million to 12,000 years ago; the Mesolithic from 12,000 to 9,000 years ago, and the Neolithic or New Stone Age from 9,000 to 6,000 years ago.

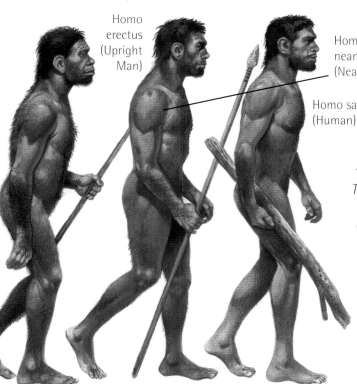

Homo erectus (Upright Man)

Homo sapiens neanderthalis (Neanderthal Man)

Homo sapiens sapiens (Human)

◀ **Evolution of humans**
*This series shows some of our ancestors, beginning with Australopithecus on the far left and ending with us humans, called by scientists Homo sapiens sapiens, on the right. The first human was called Cro-Magnon Man and lived about 30,000 years ago.*

# QUIZ

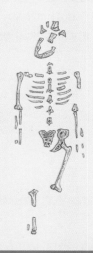

1  Early hominids made clothes from wool?

2  Early humans hunted dinosaurs: true or false?

3  Place the following ages of prehistory in the right order: the Iron Age, the Stone Age, the Bronze Age.

4  The first hominids lived in northern Canada: true or false?

5  Which of these is the most ancient: a) Java Man b) Neanderthal Man c) Cro-Magnon Man?

6  The oldest almost complete skeleton of a hominid is a) Bill b) Methusalah c) Lucy?

Answers
1. No: if they wore clothes at all they wore hide. 2. False; dinosaurs died out long before 3. Stone, Bronze then Iron 4. False  5. b)  6. c)

67

# Peoples of the world

## What are ethnic groups?

ETHNIC GROUPS ARE GROUPS of people who belong to the same race, nationality, religion, or culture. Irish people, for instance, come from the nation of Ireland or have ancestors who do. Jews are people descended from the ancient Hebrews of the Middle East and follow the Jewish religion. African Americans are descended from the West African peoples who were taken to the Americas as slaves in the 17th, 18th, and 19th centuries.

▲ Easter Island
*Huge and strange stone statues on Easter Island in the Pacific were made by Polynesian peoples thousands of years ago.*

African American

### Who are Afro-Caribbeans?
Afro-Caribbeans are descended from African slaves taken to work in the Caribbean. In the 1950s, many moved to Britain, France, and the Americas. So some British people have Afro-Caribbean parents.

### Who are Caucasians?
Police use the word Caucasian to describe white people whose ancestors came from Europe. The word comes from the Caucasus Mountains in southern Russia.

### Who lives in Africa?
In the north, in countries like Egypt, most people are Arabic. But south of the Sahara are 800 ethnic groups of black African, each with its own lifestyle and culture. Descendants of European colonists live here, too.

### Who are nomads?
Nomads are people like the Bedouins of the Sahara, Mongols of Asia, and the Masai of Africa who move around the country taking their shelters with them.

◀ Masai warrior
*The Masai are nomadic people of East Africa. Many have given up the nomadic life and now live in towns.*

▶ Maoris
*Maoris are the people who first settled in New Zealand 1,000 years ago, coming over the Pacific from the Polynesian islands in large sailing canoes.*

**▲▶ Ethnic clothes**

*In the past, people from different ethnic groups could be recognized by their traditional way of dressing, like the Polish woman in traditional costume on the right. But now most people wear modern European style like the Aboriginal children above.*

## Who lives in S. America?

In the country, some small groups of Native American peoples still survive. But in cities, there is a mix, including people descended from: Spanish settlers who came in the 1500s; marriages between Spanish settlers and Native Americans; African slaves brought here in the 18th century; and more recent European immigrants.

**▶ Oaxaca woman weaving**

*The Oaxaca of Mexico are among the few Native American peoples who survived after the Spanish arrived in the 1500s. They are famous for their woven cloth.*

## Who lives in North America?

North America was originally inhabited by Native Americans. But now most people are descended from Europeans who have come here over the centuries, from immigrants from South and Central America, to African Americans.

## Do peoples move about?

In history, whole peoples have migrated or moved huge distances. The Polynesians spread across the Pacific from South America, thousands of years ago. Asian peoples crossed into Alaska from Siberia 11,000 years ago and spread south to become Native Americans. The Anglo-Saxons of England came originally from northern Europe.

# QUIZ

1  How many people were there in the world in 1999: a) 600 million b) 1.2 billion c) 6 billion?

2  How many babies are born every minute in the world a) 2 b) 167 c) 15,000?

3  Are mestizos a) sausages b) shoes c) offspring of marriages between Native South Americans and Spanish settlers?

4  Which country has the most people: a) Russia b) India c) China?

5  What is the world's most crowded large country a) Australia b) Bangladesh c) Italy?

6  Is a kimono a) a Japanese silk gown b) a Chinese fruit c) a large lizard?

**Answers**

1. c) 2. b) 3. c) 4. c), China has more than 1.4 billion people 5. b) 6. a)

69

# The first farms

## Who were the first farmers?

EARLY PEOPLES mostly lived in small bands and moved around hunting animals and gathering food from wild plants. Then about 12,000 years ago, some people learned to herd animals such as sheep and goats to provide a ready supply of food. Others learned to sow the seeds of wild plants to grow crops. This happened at different times in different parts of the world. The earliest farms were created by the people of the Middle East around 11,000 years ago. But there were farms long ago in China, India, and Central America too.

▼ Ancient Egyptian farmers

*The development of farms led to the creation of the world's first great civilizations—including that of Ancient Egypt, where the pyramids were built. Egypt's farms were alongside the River Nile, which not only provided water, but brought rich silt soil in its floods to an area that would otherwise be desert.*

## What were the first crops?

The first crops were grown from the seeds of wild grasses which gave wheat and barley. One of the oldest known kinds of wheat is one called emmer. Vegetables such as peas were also grown on early farms.

## How did farming change people's lives forever?

For the first time, people had no need to move around looking for food. They could settle in one place and build first villages and then towns. At Jarmo in Iraq, there are the remains of 24 mud huts where 150 people lived around 11,000 years ago.

## What new skills did people learn?

To begin with farming was mixed with hunting, but the extra food meant people were free to do other tasks. Soon some people became skilled in things such as building houses and food stores, weaving cloth and making pots. They also learned how to use metals—first bronze in the Bronze Age and then iron in the Iron Age.

## What were the first inventions?

Once they were settled in farms, people began to invent all kinds of things to make life easier. They learned how to make pots from clay around 9,000 years ago. At about the same time, they learned how to grind grain into flour in shallow bowls called mortars using clublike stone pestles.

## How did they plant seeds?

At first, farmers planted seeds simply by dropping them in holes made with a stick. Then someone learned that you could get better results if you turned over the soil a bit and carved out long furrows to put the seeds in with a blade called a plough.

## When was the wheel invented?

Sometime before the wheel was invented, people may have moved heavy loads using tree trunks as rollers. The first wheels were probably slices of tree trunk with a rod or axle pushed through. A platform could rest on the axle to make a cart. By about 5,200 years ago, solid wheels made of short planks of wood bolted together were being used in Mesopotamia in the Middle East.

# QUIZ

1 Is a sickle a a) bout of feigned illness b) small black fruit c) curved blade for cutting the ears off grain?

2 What did early farmers make from wheat and barley?

3 Why did early farmers drive cattle over their grain harvest?

4 Was the farming area by the Middle East's Tigris and Euphrates rivers called the a) Grain Belt b) Fertile Crescent c) Golden Triangle?

5 5,000 years ago is a) AD 3,000 b) 7,000 BC c) 3,000 BC?

6 Is crop rotation a) spinning a horsewhip b) turning grains to face the sun c) using fields for different crops each year to preserve the soil?

**Answers**
1. c  2. Bread and beer  3. To "thresh" the grains from the stalks  4. b  5. c  6. c

# The first cities

## What were the first cities?

ONCE EARLY PEOPLE BEGAN to settle in one place in the Middle East around 11,000 years ago, families soon grew, and villages grew into cities. They were places where those who governed the land lived, craftsmen made things, and people came to buy and sell things–not only food grown in the countryside around, but metal goods, cloth, jewels, spices and much more besides.

## What's the world's oldest city?

No one knows for certain. One of the oldest is Jericho in Israel. The ruins of some of the city walls date back over 11,000 years. They were massive stone structures perhaps 23 feet (7m) tall. There were also many other cities in the Middle East at least 7,000 years ago.

## Were there any early cities in China?

Chinese civilization began more than 7,000 years ago when the Yang-Shao people built the first villages on the land between the Hwang-Ho and Wei-Ho rivers.

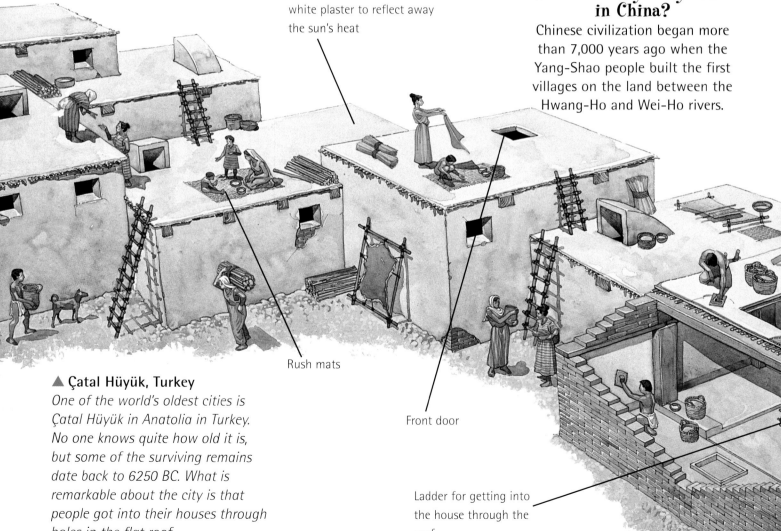

Walls and roof covered in white plaster to reflect away the sun's heat

Rush mats

Front door

Ladder for getting into the house through the roof

▲ Çatal Hüyük, Turkey
*One of the world's oldest cities is Çatal Hüyük in Anatolia in Turkey. No one knows quite how old it is, but some of the surviving remains date back to 6250 BC. What is remarkable about the city is that people got into their houses through holes in the flat roof.*

## Who built the first roof gardens?

6,000 years ago the civilization of Sumer began to flourish on the fertile land between the Tigris and Euphrates rivers in modern Iraq. Here they built the great cities of Ur and Eridu. One of the centerpieces of Ur was the ziggurat, a temple built like a step-sided pyramid—with trees and lush gardens on top.

## Where did writing begin?

Writing did not begin in any one place, but in the Middle East in Sumeria, in China and in Central America independently. The first written symbols were probably used by rulers to show their power and by city officials to record and label food and other things. One of the earliest systems of writing is "cuneiform," used in Sumer and Babylon, which used wedge-shaped marks on clay tablets.

## What were the hanging gardens of Babylon?

Babylon was first built 3,800 years ago. But it reached its height under King Nebuchadnezzar II in the 6th century BC. Its beautiful hanging gardens were one of the wonders of the world. They were planted high on a ziggurat (see left) to remind Nebuchadnezzar's queen of her mountain home.

## Who were the pharaohs?

The pharaohs were the kings of the civilization of Ancient Egypt on the banks of the River Nile. The pharaohs ruled for nearly 3,000 years, from 2920 BC, and left behind astonishing monuments to their power and wealth—not only the great pyramids and statues in the desert, but fabulous treasures in their tombs, including mummies, writing, and beautiful gold and jeweled objects.

## What is civilization?

The word civilization comes from the Latin word for city-dweller. It is the highly organized, settled way of life—complete with rules and laws, as well as writing—that came with the creation of the first cities.

Holes filled with daub (mud and straw)

Walls built with mud bricks

Framework built from wooden posts and beams

# QUIZ

1  What ancient city was carved from desert stone a) Stonehenge b) Ur c) Petra in Jordan?

2  Pyramids were built in Mexico 2,800 years ago: true or false?

3  What ancient civilization was based in Crete: a) Aztec b) Minoan c) Persian?

4  What was a chariot?

5  What would you ask a scribe to do?

6  What did the Ancient Egyptians write on?

7  Are the ruins of the ancient city of Mohenjo-Daro in a) Pakistan b) Arizona  c) Turkey?

Answers
1. c) 2. True 3. b) 4. A two-wheeled horse-drawn wagon used in battle 5. Write 6. Paper made from papyrus reed 7. a)

# Clothes and costumes

## When did people first wear clothes?

NO ONE CAN BE SURE WHEN people stopped going naked. But the first clothes were probably animal skins people wrapped round themselves to keep off the cold. It was when people began to farm and settle in villages that the earliest proper clothes were worn. At first, these were just skirts and shawls built up from twisted tufts of wool and flax. But by about 6,000 years ago, people had learned to spin and weave cloth, and sew it to make attractive clothes.

## Who were the first fashion followers?

Over 5,000 years ago, the women of Ancient Sumeria wore beautiful coloured clothes, along with fancy headdresses, and gold and silver ear-rings and necklaces, studded with jewels such as lapis-lazuli and carnelian.

## Who first wore cosmetics?

It may have been the women of Ancient Egypt, who had elaborate makeup, including eyeliner, skin powder, and lipstick. They mixed ground malachite (copper ore) and galena (lead ore) with oil to make kohl to line eyes. They made lipstick and rouge from red ocher, and also painted their nails with henna.

▼ All kinds of clothes?

*Today, fewer and fewer people wear distinctive traditional clothes. Instead, people everywhere wear the shirt, pants, skirt, and jacket made popular in North America and Europe.*

Muslim girls often wear a veil called an aba or chador covering their whole body and head

Sari, a traditional Indian dress made of silk or artificial material

Traditional turban from central Asia

Jelaba, a traditional smock worn in northern Africa.

Smocks are common in China

Baseball cap

▲ **Warm skins**
*Animal skins have provided clothes for many tens of thousands of years, especially in very cold places where wool and cotton are too thin. The Inuits and Saami people of the far north traditionally dress in skins.*

## Who invented silk?

The Chinese discovered how to make silk thread from the cocoon of the Silk moth caterpillar almost 5,000 years ago. According to legend, it was the Princess Si-ling-chi who found that the cocoon could be separated into threads in hot water. She was known thereafter as the Silk Goddess, Seine Than.

## Who first wore platform shoes?

Chopines were worn by women in Italy in the Renaissance in the 1400s. The biggest belonged to prostitutes in Venice, whose soles were built up to a height of 32 inches (80 cm) as a high as a chair.

## Who wore togas?

Togas were wraps of beautiful light cloth often worn by men in Ancient Rome over their tunics. The early togas were simple, and worn with both ends thrown over the shoulder. But in later years, they became more elaborate. Officials had togas edged in a special purple dye.

## Who first wore trousers?

The Ancient Celts of Britain wore trousers over 2,000 years ago, and so did the Chinese. Dutch and English sailors revived them in Europe in the 16th century. But it took French Revolutionaries of the 1790s to make them popular.

## What is a crinoline?

The underskirt of steel hoops Victorian ladies wore to make their dresses fuller.

# QUIZ

1  Is a jerkin a) a pickled cucumber b) a violent tennis shot c) a medieval vest?

2  The word "dungarees" comes from Indian: true or false?

3  What kind of cloth came from De Nîmes in France?

4  Where were parkas invented?

5  What do British people call a derby hat?

6  What is a tartan?

7  Some crinolines were so large, ladies had to go through double doors sideways: true or false?

8  Who wears the most armor today?

**Answers**
1. c)  2. True  3. Denim, the blue material used to make jeans  4. In the Arctic by Inuits  5. A bowler  6. A pattern of clothing linked to a Scottish clan  7. True  8. Ice hockey players

75

# Eating

## Why do we eat?

**M**OST OF THE FOOD YOU EAT is fuel, burned by your body for energy to keep you going. It gets this mainly from substances in food called carbohydrates and fats. But you also need to eat small amounts of food such as proteins to help repair and build body cells, and tiny traces of chemicals called vitamins and minerals the body cannot make itself.

### Where does food go when you eat it?

Your food goes down through your body in a long tube called the alimentary canal. When you swallow, food slides down your gullet or esphagus into the stomach, where it churns around for a few hours. Then it is squeezed into a long, coiled tube called the small intestine where nourishing parts of the food are absorbed into the blood. The rest then passes on into a larger tube called the large intestine, and the waste or faeces is pushed out through the anus.

### How long are your guts?

Your guts or intestine are so coiled that if you unwound them, they would be more than three times as long as your body.

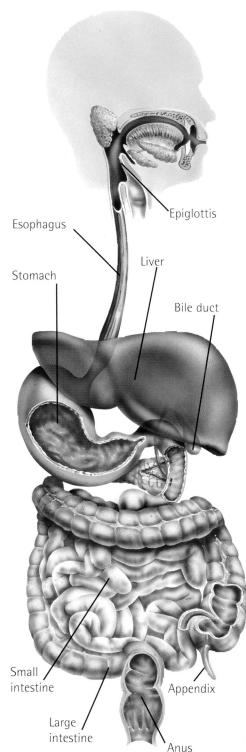

◄ **Digestive system**
*If you could see your digestive system through your body, this is what you would see. Most of the system is the alimentary canal, the long tube that takes food through your body.*

Esophagus
Epiglottis
Stomach
Liver
Bile duct
Small intestine
Appendix
Large intestine
Anus

### How is food broken down?

Food is broken into the small molecules the body needs by a process called digestion in two ways. First, food is broken up mechanically by chewing and by the squeezing muscles of your gut. Second, it is attacked chemically by acids, such as the bile and hydrochloric acid in your stomach, and by biological chemicals called enzymes, mixed in with your saliva and stomach juices.

### What are carbohydrates?

Carbohydrates are foods made of kinds of sugar like glucose and starch. Foods such as bread, rice, potatoes, and pasta, as well as sweet things, are rich in carbohydrates.

### What is fat?

Fats are greasy foods that won't dissolve in water. Some are solid, like cheese and meat fat. Others are oils. Fats are usually stored by the body as energy reserves, rather than burned up at once like carbohydrates.

◀ **A healthy diet**
*A healthy diet contains just the right amount of each kind of food your body needs, and no more. The bulk of your diet must be solid food like carbohydrates, but it must also contain enough fat, plenty of protein, and the right vitamins and minerals.*

## What food makes you grow?

To grow, your body needs proteins, the natural substances from which cells are built. Proteins are made from 20 basic chemicals called "amino acids." The body can make 12 of these. The other eight you must get by eating protein-rich food such as milk, fish, meat, eggs, and beans.

## Why are teeth different?

Different teeth do different jobs. The flat "incisors" at the front have sharp edges for slicing through food. The pointed "canine" teeth just behind are good for ripping chewy food. The big flat-topped "premolars" and "molars" toward the back of your mouth are good for grinding food into a small, mushy ball ready to be swallowed.

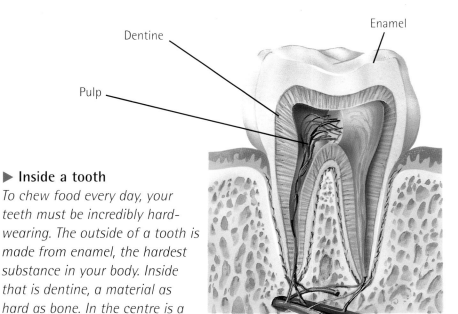

Dentine

Pulp

Enamel

▶ **Inside a tooth**
*To chew food every day, your teeth must be incredibly hard-wearing. The outside of a tooth is made from enamel, the hardest substance in your body. Inside that is dentine, a material as hard as bone. In the centre is a pulpy mass of blood and bones.*

Blood vessel

# QUIZ

1 How many teeth do most grown-ups have: a) 12 b) 32 c) 64?

2 Why does vomit taste sour? Is it because a) you've eaten sour food b) your stomach is full of acid c) vomit gets rid of body poisons?

3 Vitamin C helps your body fight infection. What foods do you get it in?

4 What is another name for the teeth you had as a baby?

5 How long can you survive without eating: a) 2 days b) 20 days c) 300 days?

6 How long can you survive without drinking: a) 2 days b) 20 days c) 300 days?

7 What kind of food is meat mostly: a) carbohydrate b) fat c) protein and fat?

**Answers**
1. b) 2. b) 3. Fresh fruit, especially oranges, plus green vegetables 4. Milk teeth 5. b) 6. a) 7. c)

# Breathing & circulation

## Why do we breathe?

JUST AS A FIRE NEEDS air to burn, so every cell in your body needs a continuous supply of oxygen to burn up the food it gets in the blood. They get their oxygen from the air you breathe in. Without oxygen your body cells quickly die—and brain cells die quickest of all. If you stopped breathing for very long, you would soon lose consciousness, your brain would be damaged and eventually you would die.

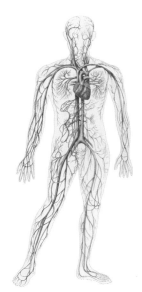

▲ **Blood vessels**
*Arteries rich in oxygen carry bright red blood. Veins which return carbon dioxide to the lungs are bluer.*

### How does your body get oxygen?

Every time you breathe in air through your nose or mouth, the air rushes down your windpipe into your lungs. Your lungs are spongey bags inside your chest, filled with millions of minute branching airways. At the end of each airway is an airsac or alveolus with walls so thin that oxygen can seep through into the tiny blood vessels wrapped around it.

### What do you breathe out?

Most of your outbreath is the air you breathed in, minus a little less oxygen. But it also contains a little waste carbon dioxide brought to the lungs from your body cells in the blood.

### How does oxygen get to each body cell?

This is what your blood circulation is for. Driven by the pumping of the heart, blood circulates through an intricate network of blood vessels all the way round the body again and again, every 90 seconds or so. As it passes through the lungs, it picks up oxygen as it washes around the airsacs. The heart then pumps this oxygen-rich blood on round the body. As the blood returns to the lungs, it carries with it the waste carbon dioxide from the cells.

### Why does the heart have two sides?

Your heart has two sides because your body has two blood circulations. The left side of the heart pumps blood through the lungs to pick up oxygen, and take it to the right of the heart. This is called pulmonary circulation. The right side pumps oxygen-rich blood around the body and back to the left of the heart. This is called the systemic circulation.

Artery taking oxygen-poor blood to the lungs

Veins bringing oxygen-rich blood back from the lungs

Right atrium, where blood is held ready to be pumped

Right ventricle, the heart's pumping chamber

## How does your heart pump?

Your heart has walls of muscle that contract automatically once a second or more. As they contract, they squeeze blood into the blood vessels. The entrances of each of the heart's two pumping chambers or ventricles have little flaps, or valves, to ensure blood can only enter and leave one way.

## Why is blood red?

Blood is ferried through the blood inside red blood cells. Red blood cells can carry oxygen because they contain a remarkable substance called hemoglobin. Hemoglobin glows bright red when it is carrying oxygen but fades to dull purple when it loses oxygen.

# QUIZ

1 There are 1,500 miles (2,400 km) of airways in your lung: true or false?

2 Your heart is in the middle of your chest, slightly to the right: true or false?

3 Blood carries food as well as oxygen to the body cells: true or false?

4 Your pulse—the rate your heart beats—is normally 300 beats a minute: true or false?

5 What are the major blood vessels that carry blood away from the heart called?

6 Are the tiniest blood vessels called: a) filigrees b) venioles c) capillaries?

7 Smoking damages which body tissue?

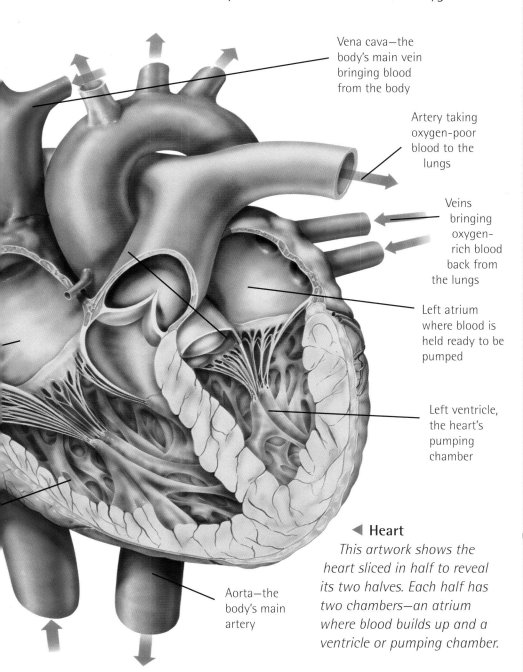

Vena cava—the body's main vein bringing blood from the body

Artery taking oxygen-poor blood to the lungs

Veins bringing oxygen-rich blood back from the lungs

Left atrium where blood is held ready to be pumped

Left ventricle, the heart's pumping chamber

Aorta—the body's main artery

◀ **Heart**
*This artwork shows the heart sliced in half to reveal its two halves. Each half has two chambers—an atrium where blood builds up and a ventricle or pumping chamber.*

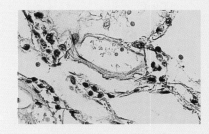

# Moving

## Why do you have bones in your body?

WITHOUT BONES, YOU WOULD FLOP on the floor like jelly. Your bones make the strong, rigid framework called the skeleton that supports your body. It not only provides an anchor for your muscles, but supports your skin and and other tissues. It also provides a protective casing for your heart, brain, and other organs.

### How many bones do you have ?

A baby's skeleton has more than 300 bones, but some fuse together as it grows. You probably have 213 bones—though some people have extra bones in their back.

### What's inside a bone?

The very center of many bones is a core of soft, jelly material called bone marrow. This where your blood cells are made.

### Why are bones strong?

Their tough outer casing combines two materials—one that makes them flexible and another that makes them stiff. The flexible material is strong, stretchy strands called collagen. The stiff material is hard deposits of the minerals calcium and phosphate.

### Why don't bones weigh you down?

Bones are incredibly light despite their strength because they are full of holes. Inside the casing is a crisscross honeycomb structure of struts called trabeculae.

### What are joints?

Joints are places where two bones meet. A few joints, such as those in the skull, are completely rigid. But most joints allow the bones to move, and the end of each bone is shaped to allow it to move in a particular way. The knee is a hinge joint that lets the lower leg swing back and forward. The hip is a ball and socket joint that lets you rotate your leg all round.

### What do muscles do?

Muscles make parts of your body move. They work by making themselves shorter, so that they pull things together. When the muscle on the front of your upper arm gets shorter, it pulls up your forearm.

### Are there different kinds of muscle?

The outside of your skeleton is covered in muscles called skeletal muscles that you use to make your body move. But there are also muscles inside your body called involuntary muscles that move food through your guts and control your blood flow without you being aware of it. A third kind of muscle works your heart.

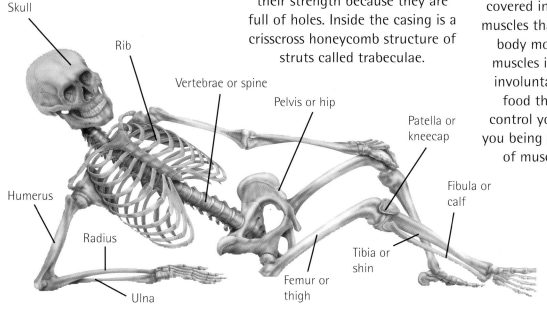

Skull
Rib
Vertebrae or spine
Pelvis or hip
Patella or kneecap
Humerus
Fibula or calf
Radius
Tibia or shin
Femur or thigh
Ulna

◀ Skeleton
*Your skeleton is a tough, light framework of more than 200 bones.*

## ▼ Inside a muscle

*A muscle is made of bundles of fibres, each made of strands called fibrils, which are in turn made up of myofibrils.*

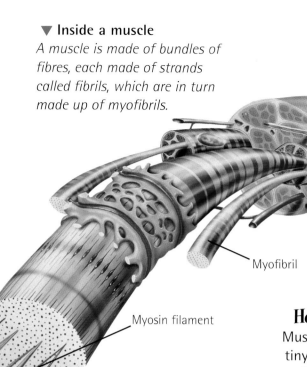

Muscle fiber

Fibril

Myofibril

Myosin filament

Actin filament

## Why do muscles work in pairs?

Muscles work in pairs because they can only pull themselves shorter. They need a partner working the opposite way to pull them out again. On your upper arm, you have biceps muscles at the front, which shorten to lift your forearm. You have triceps muscles at the back to pull it lower again.

## How do muscles work?

Muscles are made of bundles of tiny fibers that get thicker and shorter when the muscle is working. Each of the fibers is made of interlocking strands of two materials, actin and myosin. The myosin has little chemical hooks that twist and tug on the actin to make the muscle shorter.

## How are bones and muscles attached?

Muscles are attached to bones by tough cords called tendons. Bones are bound together by tough cords called ligaments.

### Different kinds of joint

Ball and socket joints like the shoulder and hip allow free movement in many directions.

In your thumbs, two-saddle-shaped bone ends fit snugly to combine strength and free movement.

The swivel joint between your skull and spine lets you turn your head to the left and right.

Hinge joints like those in the knee and elbow swing only two ways like a door, but are strong.

81

# Seeing

## How do you see things?

**Y**OUR EYES ARE A LITTLE like tiny TV cameras. At the front is a lens called the cornea–the disk in the center of your eye. This projects a picture onto an array of light-sensitive cells called the retina lining the back of your eye. The retina then sends signals to your brain.

## How do you see when it's dark?

In order to see well in dim light, your pupils open wider to let in more light. In the dark, it gets up to 16 times bigger. The sensitivity of the retina increases too, by up to 100,000 times. But the retina becomes less sensitive and the pupil narrows in very bright light. Even so, very bright light can damage the eyes, which is why you should never look directly at the sun.

## Why do we have two eyes?

Each eye gives a slightly different view of the same thing. The nearer a thing is, the greater the difference between the view. These slight differences combine in the brain to give us an impression of 3D depth and solidity, and allow you to judge easily just how far away things are.

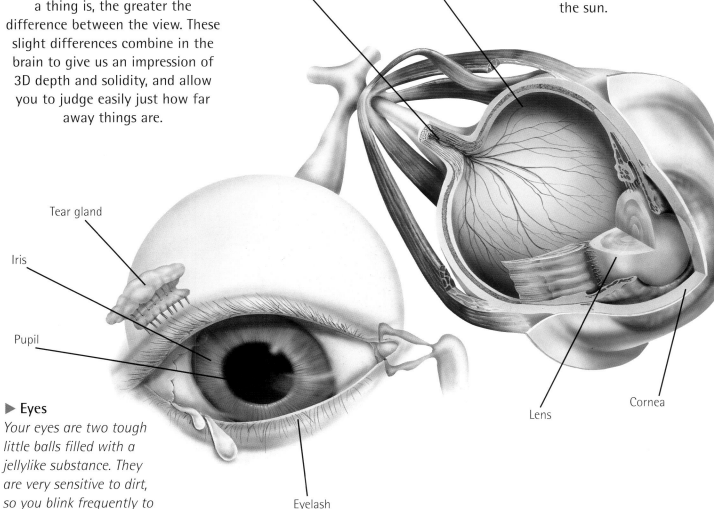

Optic nerve to the brain

Retina (light-sensitive layer)

Tear gland

Iris

Pupil

Lens

Cornea

▶ **Eyes**
*Your eyes are two tough little balls filled with a jellylike substance. They are very sensitive to dirt, so you blink frequently to wipe away dust, and they are washed by tears.*

Eyelash

82

## ▶ Color mix
*All the colors you see are contained in white daylight. If you spin this wheel of color, the colors would mix to look white.*

## What are rods and cones?
Rods and cones are the two kinds of light-sensitive cell in your retina. Rods tell you how bright light is. Cones tell you what color it is. Rods are much more sensitive than cones and work even in dim light. Cones don't work well in dim light, which is why colors look gray at night.

## How do you see in color?
It was once thought that there are three kinds of cones in the eye—some sensitive to red light, some to green, and others to blue. So some scientists think you see colors simply as different mixtures of these three "primary" colors. Others think there are pairs of cones sensitive to blue and yellow, red and green, and the color you see depends on which half of the pair is stimulated most by the light.

## What's in your eyeball?
Eyes are filled with a jellylike substance called vitreous humor, which is very clear to let you see well.

## What are primary colors?
Primary colors are three basic colors that can be mixed in different proportions to make every other color. The primary colors of light are blue, green, and red. But when mixing paint you use three different primary colors—yellow, magenta (a kind of purply red), and cyan (a greeny blue).

## What is short sight?
Not everyone sees equally well. Short sight is when your eyeball is slightly stretched out, so you can only see things nearby clearly without glasses or contact lenses. Long sight is when you only see distant things clearly.

## What is your iris?
The iris is the ring around the dark center or pupil of your eye. It contracts or expands to open the pupil wider, or close it.

## ◀ Flipped flower
*As rays of light focus through the cornea, they cross over. So the picture in your eye is flipped upside down, though your brain sees it as normal.*

# Hearing

## How do you hear?

SOUND REACHES YOUR EAR AS VIBRATIONS in the air. Your ear flap funnels sound into a tube into your head called the ear canal. Inside, the sound hits a taut wall of thin skin called the eardrum and makes it vibrate like a drum. As the eardrum vibrates, it rattles three little bones called ossicles, which knock against the "cochlea," deep inside the ear. The cochlea is filled with fluid, and as it is knocked waves run through the fluid, and the waves waggle hairs attached to nerves. The waggling of the hairs tells your brain about the sound.

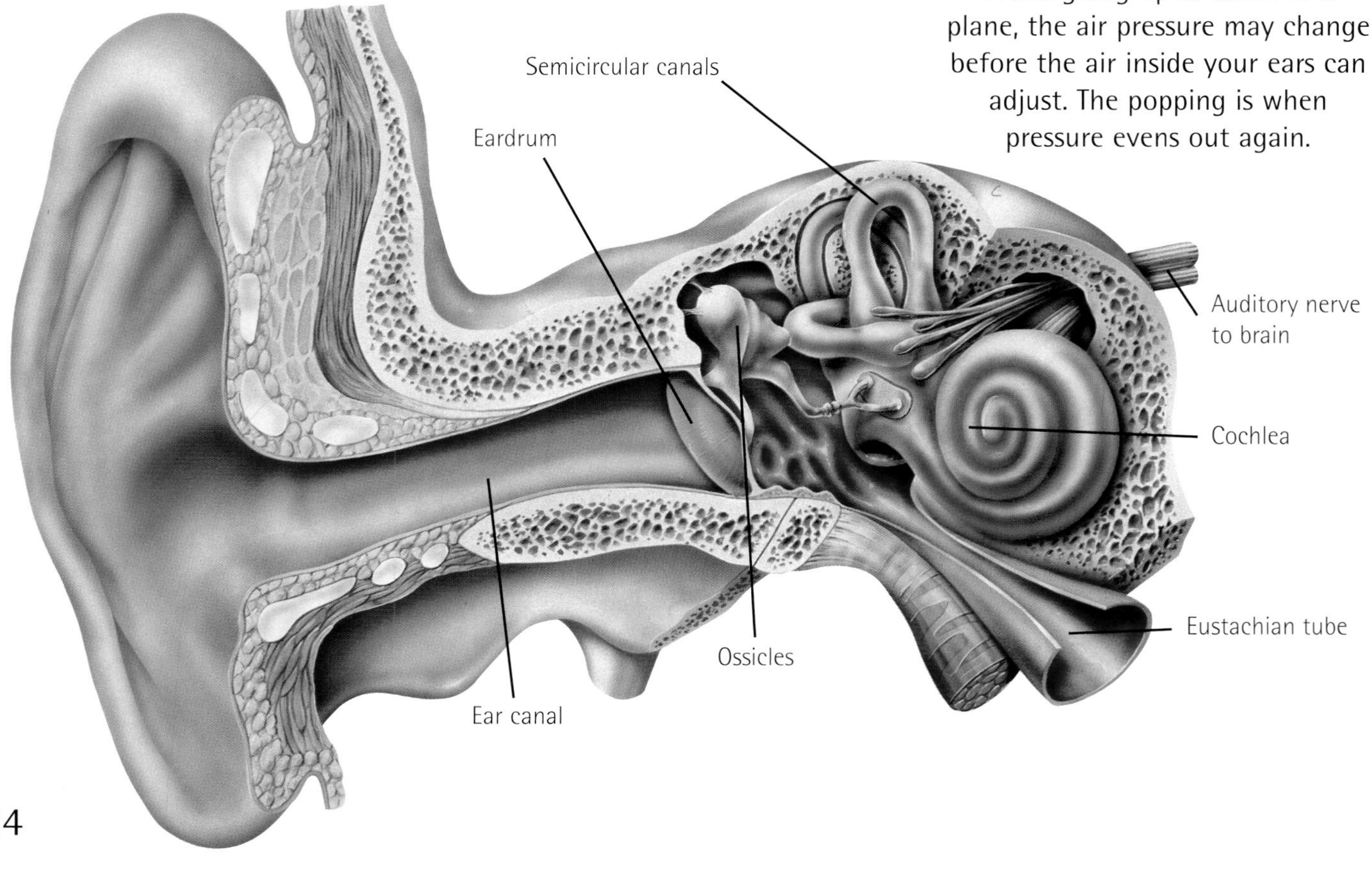

### Why do you have two ears?

So that you can tell which direction a sound is coming from. You can pinpoint sound because a sound to the left of you is slightly louder in your left ear than in the right ear, and vice versa.

### What is earwax?

Earwax is a yellow-brown waxy substance made in the glands lining the ear canal. Its purpose is to trap dirt and germs and prevent them getting into the inner ear. It is slowly eased out of the ear.

### Why do ears pop?

When going up or down in a plane, the air pressure may change before the air inside your ears can adjust. The popping is when pressure evens out again.

▼ Inside the ear
*The flap of skin on the side of your head is only the entrance to the real ear. Inside are all the complex mechanisms of the middle ear, designed to pick up the faintest vibrations in the air and amplify them enough for the hearing nerve to respond to.*

Semicircular canals

Eardrum

Auditory nerve to brain

Cochlea

Eustachian tube

Ossicles

Ear canal

## ▶ Inside the cochlea

*The vibrations of a sound are amplified (made much bigger) by the time they reach the cochlea of the inner ear, but they are still very tiny. So inside the cochlea is a remarkably sensitive mechanism that picks up every slight movement of the fluid.*

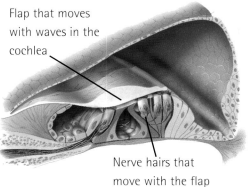

Flap that moves with waves in the cochlea

Nerve hairs that move with the flap

## How is sound measured?

Sound is measured in decibels. Decibels go up geometrically—that is, three decibels is twice as loud as two and four twice as loud as three, and so on.

## How loud is a pin dropping?

About ten decibels—just about the quietest sound you can hear. A whisper is about 20 decibels. Some animals hear even quieter sounds.

## How loud is a jet?

Close up, a jet engine is about 140 decibels. This kind of noise is genuinely painful to the ears, and can do lasting damage. Indeed, any continuous sound over 90 decibels can be damaging.

## How do your ears help you balance?

Next to the cochlea is a cluster of three fluid filled rings called semi-circular canals. These canals act like tiny spirit levels, telling you when you are tilting one way or the other, as the fluid moves inside the canal.

## What are the ossicles?

The ossicles are three linked bones in the middle ear. They all have Latin names and a simple English equivalent: hammer or malleus, anvil or incus, stirrup or stapes.

Hammer

Anvil

Stirrup

## ▲ Ossicles

*Sounds are transmitted through the middle ear by the tiny ossicle bones. The hammer bangs against the anvil like a blacksmith's hammer on his anvil. The stirrup gets its name because it is shaped like a rider's stirrup.*

# QUIZ

1 The cochlea is named after the snail: true or false?

2 The nerve hairs inside the cochlea are called a) the ear trumpet of Obi b) Copper's flute c) the organ of Corti?

3 Is the scientific name for your earflap: a) pinna b) sinna c) dinna?

4 Humans can hear much higher-pitched sounds than dogs: true or false?

5 Sound travels through the air in a) waves b) straight lines c) little lumps?

6 What is the loudest sound in space?

7 The pitch of a sound is measured in a) Hertz b) Akes c) Paynes?

8 Sound travels faster through water than air: true or false?

9 The ear is connected to the top of your throat: true or false?

# Taste, smell, and touch

## How do you taste things?

YOU TASTE THINGS BOTH WITH taste buds on your tongue and also by using other senses. Your taste buds can only detect the difference between sweet food, salty food, sour food, and bitter food. But when you eat, other sensations–heat and cold, texture, and especially smell–also come into play. It is these extra sensations that help you tell the difference between a huge range of foods.

▲ **Taste bud**
*The taste buds contain clusters of cells with hairs on the end. When these hairs are washed over by saliva, they react if the saliva contains the right taste.*

▼ **Cheese tastes**
*Taste buds can detect little real difference between all these cheeses. But other senses such as smell combine with taste to reveal the range of flavors.*

### What are taste buds?
Taste buds are clusters of special cells set in tiny wells in your tongue—so tiny that there are 10,000 of them altogether. As you chew, tiny particles of food dissolve in saliva and trickle down into the taste buds. Each taste bud reacts to a particular kind of taste—sweet, salty, sour, or bitter. If the food contains the right flavor, the taste bud is triggered and it immediately sends off a message down nerves to your brain.

### Where do you taste sweet and sour things?
Your taste buds are hidden away inside tiny bumps on your tongue called papillae. Taste buds that respond to sweet tastes are on the tip of the tongue. Salty flavors are detected just behind on the sides of the tongue. Sour things set off taste buds on the sides of your tongue farther back. Really bitter tastes hit the back of your tongue.

### How do you smell?
Smells are tiny particles in the air. As you breathe in, some of these particles travel up your nose and dissolve in the mucus. They then drift toward a small patch at the top inside called the olfactory epithelium. This tiny patch is packed with ten million smell receptors. These smell receptors react to chemicals dissolved in the mucus and send messages to your brain.

## How do you feel things?

You feel things touch your skin because your skin is packed with different kinds of receptors that can tell you whether things are hard or soft, hot or cold, rough or smooth to the touch.

## Where can you feel things?

There are sense receptors in almost every part of your skin. But some places, like your hands and face, have lots of receptors and so are very sensitive. Other places on the body—the small of your back, for instance—have very few and so are not so sensitive.

## How do you know how hard someone's pushing?

When someone touches you, the receptors in the skin send off signals to your brain. The harder the touch, the faster the nerves send signals.

## Which parts of the body are most sensitive to heat?

Your elbows and feet are more sensitive to heat than many other parts of the body. This is why mothers sometimes test the bathwater for babies to make sure it isn't too hot by putting their elbow in the water.

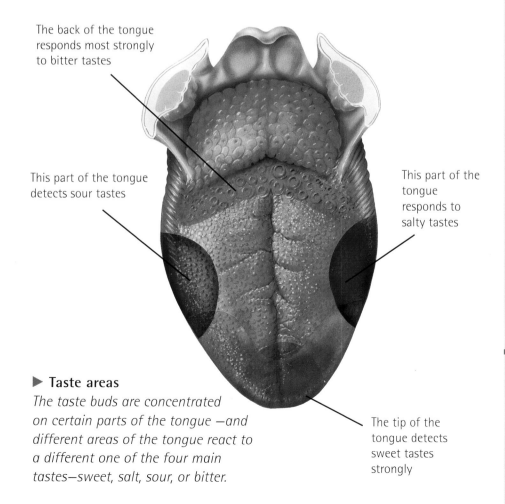

The back of the tongue responds most strongly to bitter tastes

This part of the tongue detects sour tastes

This part of the tongue responds to salty tastes

The tip of the tongue detects sweet tastes strongly

▶ **Taste areas**
*The taste buds are concentrated on certain parts of the tongue —and different areas of the tongue react to a different one of the four main tastes—sweet, salt, sour, or bitter.*

# QUIZ

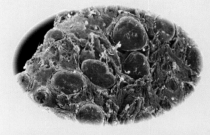

1 Sometimes you can't taste things if your nose is blocked with a cold: true or false?

2 By the age of 20, you will have lost 20% of your sense of smell: true or false?

3 Dog's noses are a) 100 times more sensitive than humans b) 10,000 times c) 1 million times?

4 Babies have a better sense of smell: true or false?

5 It is possible to smell up to 100 feet (30m) underwater: true or false?

6 Sense receptors connect to which part of the brain: a) the midbrain b) the brain stem c) the cortex?

7 Taste buds last only a day: true or false?

**Answers**
1. True 2. True 3. b) 4. True 5. False; you can't smell underwater. 6. c) 7. False; taste buds last a week before the body replaces them

# Thinking

## What is a brain?

YOUR BRAIN IS an amazing package of 100 billion tiny nerve cells, each connected with up to 25,000 others. This huge number of interconnecting nerve cells is what makes your brain clever-enabling it to do everything from analyzing all the signals coming from your senses to controlling your body-and thinking.

The cerebral cortex receives signals form the senses and sends signals to move parts of your body

Basal ganglia

The frontal lobe of the cerebrum is involved in thinking and planning.

Cerebellum

Hippocampus

Pituitary gland controls many important body hormones

Brain stem

▲ **Inside the brain**
*All the brain looks quite similar to start with, but a closer look reveals a varied structure. It has two halves or hemispheres, left and right, linked by a bundle of nerves called the corpus callosum. In the center are a collection of different structures, each with its own task.*

### What goes on in the brain?
Different things happen in different parts of the brain. The center of the brain is right at the top of the neck where nerves from the spine join it. This is where body functions you don't have to think about—like breathing and heart rate—are controlled. Just behind this is the "cerebellum," which controls balance and coordination. Wrapped around the outside is the cerebrum where you think, and complex tasks such as speaking and actions you decide on are controlled.

### What is the nervous system?
The nervous system is your body's hot line carrying messages from the brain to every organ and muscle in your body—and sending back a constant stream of information to your brain about the world both inside and outside your body. It is made from long strings of special nerve cells or neurons.

### What is the central nervous system?
The brain and the spinal cord (the bundle of nerves that runs through the middle of your backbone) together make what is called the Central Nervous System, or CNS. All the body's nerves radiate out from the CNS in branches. This is why severe damage to the spine can make someone paralyzed.

## Where in your brain do you see things?

All your senses are received in a part of the brain called the cortex, which is like the brain's rind, the outer layer of the brain at the top.

The part of your brain that registers what you see is called the "visual cortex." This is right at the back of the brain.

## How does a brain appear?

It looks like a large, soggy, pinkish gray walnut on the outside. This is because the outer part of the brain is made of masses of nerves called gray matter, which are wrinkled up to get as much inside your head as possible.

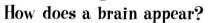

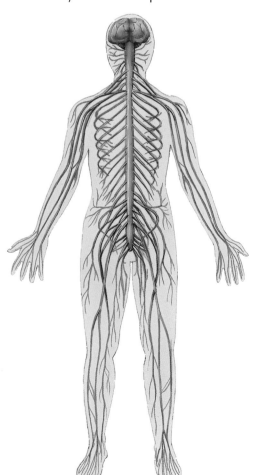

▲ **Juggling**
*Skills like juggling, which require tremendous coordination are gradually programmed into the cerebellum at the back of the brain.*

## What's the difference between the brain's two halves?

The left side of your brain controls the right side of your body; the right side controls the left. Most people are right-handed because the left side of the brain is dominant. In left-handed people, the right side of the brain is dominant. Since the part of the brain that controls speech is in the left of the brain, and the part of the brain that controls awareness of space is in the right, some people believe left-handed people are likely to be good at art and design.

◀ **Nerves in the body**
*Nerves link your brain to every part of the body. Like branches on a tree, the nerves spread out from the Central Nervous System (the brain and spinal cord). Motor nerves control movement. Sensory nerves send signals back to the brain. Sensory and motor nerves are usually paired.*

# QUIZ

1 The small club-shaped part of the brain center that controls moods, willpower and learning is called the a) hippopotamus b) hippocampus c) cortex?

2 The brain is the only part of the body that can survive without oxygen: true or false?

3 Boys' brains are bigger in relation to their bodies than girls': true or false?

4 The tiny gaps between the ends of nerves are called a) gates b) prolapses c) synapses?

5 The brain goes to sleep when you do: true or false?

**Answers**
1. b) 2. False; even a few minutes without damages the brain 3. False; the reverse is true 4. c) 5. False

# Growing

## How do you grow bigger?

**Y**OUR BODY IS MADE UP FROM MILLIONS of tiny packets called cells, nearly all of them so tiny they can be seen only under a powerful microscope. You grow as these cells divide in two again and again to make new cells. This is called cell multiplication and happens most when you're young. You look young because most of your body is made from new cells.

### What makes you grow?
You grow bigger mainly because the pituitary gland in your brain sends out a chemical in the blood called "growth hormone." When this hormone is released into the blood from time to time, it tells body cells to divide and multiply.

▼ **Body changes**
*Most people in the richer parts of the world live until they are 70 or more, and some live until they are 100. During their lives, their body will have gone through many changes, gradually growing during childhood, then slowly deteriorating once they are adults.*

You stop growing when you are and adult, and may have children of your own

At puberty, the body changes shape and sexual organs begin to mature

As people get older, they begin to slow down and get less fit and active

During childhood, legs and arms grow longer and adult teeth grow

Old people may become quite frail and their senses are weaker

A two-year old is about half the height it will be when an adult

Babies often learn to crawl before they take their first tottering steps

90

## What is puberty?

You are born with sexual or reproductive organs—the organs that enable you to have children when you are an adult. Puberty is the time of your life when they develop in the right way for you to have children. Puberty comes at different ages in different people. Girls typically reach puberty at 11 or 12. Boys reach it at 13 or so.

## What happens at puberty?

Puberty is the time when your body begins to change from a child's into an adult's. A girl begins to grow breasts and her hips become wider, and she grows hair around her genitals. Eventually she starts her monthly periods of menstruation. A boy's testes begin to grow and produce sperm. He begins to grow hair on his chin and his voice deepens.

## What happens when you grow old?

By the time you are 20 or so, you are fully grown. From then on, your body starts to slowly deteriorate. People age at different rates, but by the time you are 65 or so, you will be less fit, and less able to run and jump. Your hair will probably be gray or white. You may be bald if you are a man. Your skin will be wrinkled. You may stoop. You will certainly find all your senses less sharp. All the same, all body cells except for nerve cells are continually being renewed, even when you old.

1. Before cell division begins, each chromosome is copied, and the two copies coil up into dark rods that join to make an X-shaped pair

2. The pairs of chromosomes line up across the center of the cell. They stick on to tiny threads that grow across the cell

3. The threads begin tugging in opposite directions. The pairs split in half, and each half is pulled to the opposite end of the cell

4. A new nucleus starts to form around the cluster of chromosomes at each end of the thread. Each cluster of chromosomes is identical

5. A membrane grows around the two new nuclei, and eventually the old cell divides down the middle to create two brand new cells

▲ How cells grow

*New human cells are made when old cells split in half. This is how your body grows when you are young, and how body cells that are worn out are replaced by new ones. The process of cell division is called mitosis, and ensures that each new cell is identical and gets a copy of the cell's instructions or chromosomes.*

# QUIZ

1  The part of your body that grows quickest until you are five is a) the brain  b) the legs c) the tongue?

2  A doctor who specializes in treating children is called a a) neurologist  b) pediatrician c) pedologist?

3  Your brain goes on growing all your life: true or false?

4  The rate at which you grow is controlled by a chemical released by the pituitary gland in your brain: true or false?

5  The tallest man who ever lived was nearly 9 feet (2.7m) tall: true or false?

6  What part of your body is almost as big when you are baby as it will be when you are an adult?

Answers
1. a) 2. b) 3. False 4. True
5. True
6. Your head

91

What's the biggest creature that
ever lived on land?

Where does sand
come from?

Was Australia ever
joined to Africa?

What is a wadi?

Do glaciers ever
melt?

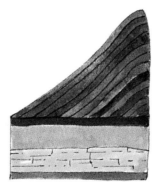

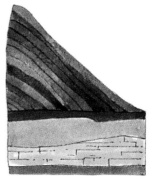

How do we know
dinosaurs existed?

Could we ever visit the center of the Earth?

Was New York ever in the tropics?

# Earth

How does frost break rock?

How long do earthquakes last?

When did the first humans appear?

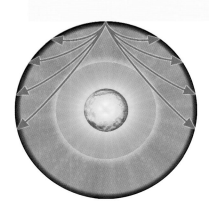

How hot is it in the Earth?

# Earth's history

## How old is the Earth?

Earth formed 4.55 billion years ago

Archean

Precambrian

Proterozoic

THE EARTH IS ABOUT 4.6 BILLION YEARS OLD. Scientists know this from analyzing meteorites—lumps of rocky debris that have fallen to Earth from space and probably formed at the same time as the Earth. They can tell the age of a meteorite by studying atoms in it. When the meteorite formed, certain atoms in it began to break up at a constant rate. By analyzing just how far they have broken up scientists can tell exactly how old the meteorite is. This is called radioactive dating.

### How is Earth's history divided up?

Just as the day is divided into hours, minutes, and seconds, geologists divide the Earth's history into different time Periods. The longest are eons, which are hundreds of millions of years long. The shortest are Chrons, just a few thousand years long. In between come Eras, Periods, Epochs, and Ages.

### What do we know about Earth's early history?

We know only a little about the first four billion years of Earth's history, called the Precambrian because fossils from that time are rare. But we know a great deal about the last 590 million years, since the beginning of the Cambrian Period, and this is split into 11 Periods.

### How can you tell how old a rock is?

Many rocks form from mud and other sediments on seabeds and riverbeds. When living things die, their remains are sometimes preserved in sediments like these. Because different plants and animals lived at different Periods in Earth's history, geologists can tell how long ago the rocks formed from the fossils they contain.

### When did the dinosaurs live?

The dinosaurs first appeared during the Triassic Period, about 220 million years ago. They became widespread over the next 150 million years, during the Jurassic and Cretaceous Periods. Then about 65 million years ago, they suddenly died out—perhaps because a huge asteroid struck the Earth and turned it cold.

Key:
1. Jellyfish
2. Trilobite
3. Acanthodian (jawed fish)
4. Cooksonia (early land plant)
5. Ichthyostega (early amphibian)
6. Dimetrodon (early mammal-like reptile
7. Anteosaurus
8. Herrerasaurus (early dinosaur)
9. Pterandon (early flying reptile)
10. Cephalopod (squidlike shellfish)
11. Brachiosaurus (dinosaur)
12. Crusafontia (small mammal)
13. Merychippus (early horse)
14. Proconsul (great ape)
15. Homo sapiens (early man)

## ▼ Earth's history

*This illustration shows the major time Periods of Earth's history and some of the characteristic fossil creatures and plants that help geologists identify rocks from each of these different Periods.*

**Key to Periods:**

*Archean: 4,600-2,500 million years ago (mya)*
*Proterozoic 2,500-590 mya*
*Cambrian 590 mya*
*Ordovician 505 mya*
*Silurian 438 mya*
*Devonian 408 mya*
*Carboniferous 360 mya*
*Permian 286 mya*
*Triassic 284 mya*
*Jurassic 213 my.a*
*Cretaceous 144 mya*
*Tertiary 65 mya*
*Quaternary 2 mya*

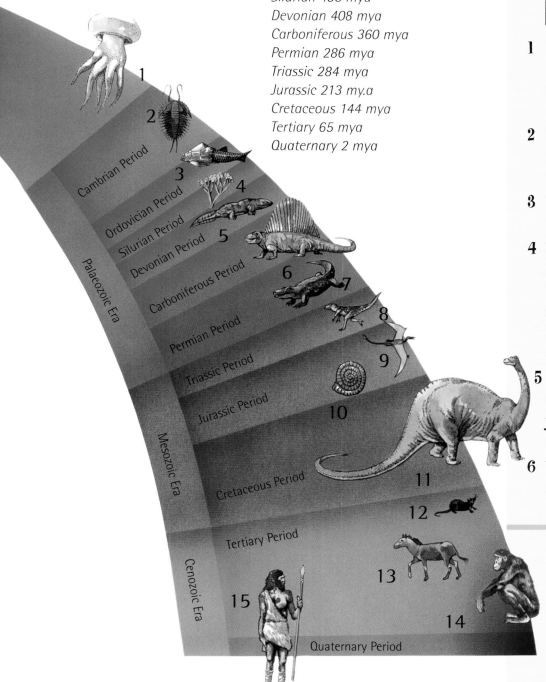

# QUIZ

**1** Is a meteorite a a) ball of rock from space b) kind of ancient rock c) kind of dinosaur?

**2** The Earth formed from the remains of an old star: true or false?

**3** What was the first living thing on Earth?

**4** What period in Earth's history did the swamps that gave us coal form in:
a) Precambrian
b) Carboniferous
c) Quaternary?

**5** How old is the oldest rock ever found a) 38,000 years b) 380 million years c) 3.8 billion years?

**6** When did the first humans appear?

95

# Fossils

## What are fossils?

FOSSILS ARE THE RELICS of plants and animals that have been preserved for many thousands or millions of years, usually in stone. They may be the remains of living things–bones, shells, eggs, seeds, and so on. Or they may just be signs, such as footprints or scratchmarks, left behind.

▼ **Fossils**

*There are many different ways in which once living things can be fossilized.*
**Key:** *1. Spider in amber, the hardened resin of ancient trees*
*2. Leaves turned to carbon*
*3. Trace fossil: footprint preserved in hardened mud*
*4. Fossilized shark's teeth*
*5. Trilobite: ancient shellfish*
*6. Petrified (turned to stone) logs*

## What is the oldest fossil?

The oldest fossils, but for microscopic traces of bacteria, are "stromatolites." These are fossils of giant pizzalike mats, made by colonies of billions of microscopic cyanobacteria. Some of these date back more than 3 billion years!

## How do fossils form?

When an animal dies, its soft parts rot away quickly, but if its bones or shell are buried quickly in mud, they may eventually turn to stone. When a shellfish dies and sinks to the seafloor, its old shell gets buried in mud. Over millions of years, water trickling through the mud dissolves away the shell, but minerals in the water fill its place, making a perfect cast.

## How do scientists tell a fossil's age?

From the rock it is found in. They know how old rocks are relative to each other because layers of rock form on top of each other, so the lowest layers are oldest. Measuring the fossil's radioactivity gives a more precise date.

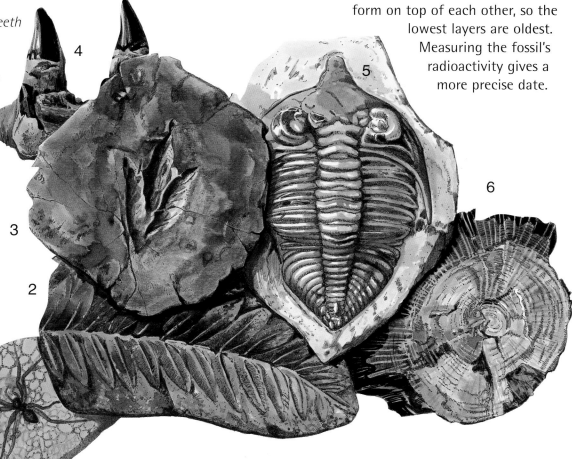

▼ Big lizard

*Iguanadon was one of the first dinosaurs identified, by the fossil hunter Gideon Mantell in the 1820s. Mantell found a fossilized claw of the iguanodon, and realized that it was very similar to that of a modern iguana (a kind of lizard)—only twenty times as big! Mantell thought it had four legs like an iguana. We now know it only had two.*

## Why do geologists study fossils?

The simplest way to tell the age of a rock is from the fossils it contains. Many species only lived at certain times during Earth's history. So if a rock contains a species that dates from a certain time, the rock must have formed at that time too. Useful fossil species for dating are called index fossils. These index fossils include certain ancient kinds of shellfish called trilobites, graptolites, brachiopods, crinoids, ammonites, and belemnites.

## What do fossils tell us?

It is from the study of fossils that fossil scientists have learned how plants and animals evolved on Earth. They have found that most species only lived for a short time, before being superseded by another better adapted to the conditions of the time.

## How do we know dinosaurs existed?

Because they left behind a huge number of their fossilized remains. No one knew what they were for a long time. In China, people thought they belonged to dragons. Then in the 1820s an English naturalist named William Buckland recognized them for what they were. Now hundreds of species of dinosaur have been identified from fossils, and recently, a clutch of dinosaur eggs was discovered with the babies inside.

## What's the biggest creature that ever lived on land?

The largest dinosaurs were the plant-eating sauropods, which had long necks for browsing on trees. The biggest may have been the brachiosaurus, which was at least 46 feet (14m) tall and 80 feet (25m) long—four times as tall as an elephant and six times as long.

# QUIZ

1 What was the biggest predatory dinosaur that ever lived?

2 There once were flying dinosaurs as big as airplanes: true or false?

3 There were creatures on land long before there were any in the sea: true or false?

4 Coal is the fossilized remains of swamp plants: true or false?

5 Woolly mammoths (large, hairy elephantlike creatures) were found preserved in a) sugar b) ice c) sand?

6 Which of these shelled creatures was related to squids: a) ammonite b) cockle c) brachiopod?

Answers

1. Tyrannosaurus Rex 2. True 3. False 4. True 5. b) 6. c)

# Continental drift

## Have the continents always been the same?

NO. THEY MAY LOOK VERY FIXED but the continents are moving slowly all the time. Sometimes they crunch together. Sometimes they break apart in the middle. But they are always drifting about the world, like ice floes on a pond. This is called continental drift.

### How fast are the continents moving?

The speed continents move varies from place to place. North America is drifting away from Europe at about an inch (2.5cm) a year—the same rate a fingernail grows. This might seem slow but over millions of years, it can take continents thousands of miles.

### Why could South America and Africa fit together like a jigsaw puzzle?

Because they were once joined together—along with all the other continents—in a giant supercontinent that geologists call Pangea. About 200 million years ago, Pangea began to break up, and the fragments have drifted apart to form today's continents.

### What happens when continents crunch together?

The edge of one continent may well be crumpled up. These crumples or folds form high mountain ranges. The Himalayan Mountains were thrown up where India crashed into Asia. Indeed, the Himalayas are getting higher, because India is still pushing into Asia.

### Is it just the continents that move?

No. The whole of the Earth's surface is broken into 20 or so giant fragments called tectonic plates, and all of these move around. The continents are simply carried on top of these moving plates, like cargo on a raft.

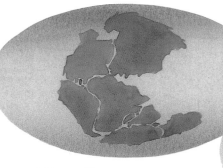

220 mya The continents were joined together as Pangea

▶ Pangea
*The map of the world has been changing over time. 220 million years ago (mya), there was just one supercontinent, Pangea, and one giant ocean Panthalassa. By analyzing the alignment of magnetic particles in rocks (which set pointing North like compasses), geologists have traced how the continents have drifted since.*

200 mya Pangea split into two landmasses, Gondwanaland in the south and Laurasia in the north

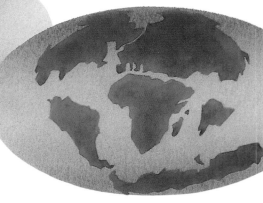

135 mya The South Atlantic opened between South America and Africa. India broke off and drifted toward Asia

# QUIZ

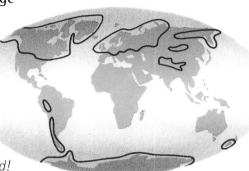

**► Ice cover in the Ice Age**
*At times during Earth's history, in cold periods called Ice Ages, many parts of the world have been covered in thick ice. Because continents have drifted, even the Sahara was once glaciated!*

## Was New York ever in the tropics?

Yes. 250 million years ago, the place where New York is now was on the equator, and it was a boiling hot desert. It was in this hot desert that the sandstone formed that gave New York its famous brownstone houses. 300 million years ago, New York was a steamy swamp.

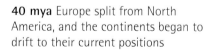

**40 mya** Europe split from North America, and the continents began to drift to their current positions

## Why do the continents move?

Probably because they are carried on by moving currents of molten rock in the Earth's interior. Just as bubbles rise to the surface in boiling soup, so giant streams of molten rock rise up through the Earth's hot interior. When they come up beneath the surface, these "convection currents" spread out sideways, carrying the continents with them.

## Was Australia ever joined to Africa?

Yes, about 200 million years ago the north coast of Australia was joined to the south east coast of Africa.

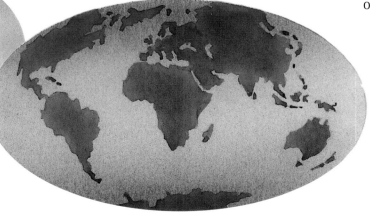

**The future** The Pacific will shrink and the Atlantic will get wider. Africa will split along the Great Rift Valley in the east

1 Million of years ago you could have walked from Spain to Newfoundland in a few hours: true or false?

2 What continent was once attached to the south coast of Australia?

3 Which two continents crashed together to form the Alps?

4 The San Andreas fault in California is the gap between two tectonic plates: true or false?

5 Tides in the sea occur because the continents are moving: true or false?

6 There were once dinosaurs in Antarctica: true or false?

7 Was the Sahara always a desert?

Answers
1.True 2. Antarctica 3. Europe and Africa 4. True 5. False 6. True 7. No

# Structure of the Earth

## What's inside the Earth?

THE HARDY, ROCKY SURFACE OF THE EARTH, called the crust, is just a thin shell. Inside, the Earth gets hotter and hotter until at the very center the temperature reaches 12,600°F (7,000°C)–hotter than the surface of the Sun. So just beneath the crust, there is an ocean of half-molten rock thousands of miles deep called the mantle. Beneath this, in the Earth's center is an outer core of molten iron and nickel. In the inner core, pressure is so intense that the metal cannot melt despite the heat.

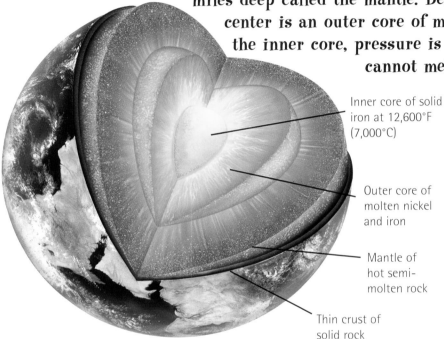

Inner core of solid iron at 12,600°F (7,000°C)

Outer core of molten nickel and iron

Mantle of hot semi-molten rock

Thin crust of solid rock

▲ **Inside the Earth**
*Beneath the thin shell called the crust, the Earth churns and bubbles like soup, and at the boundary of the Earth's core there may be continents and oceans like those on the surface.*

### How big is the Earth's crust?

The Earth's crust is surprisingly thin. Proportionally it is not much thicker than the skin on an apple. It is thickest beneath the continents. But even here it is no more than 40 miles (68km) thick at most. It is thinnest beneath the oceans, often less than 5 miles (8km) thick.

### How do we know what the Earth is like inside?

From the vibrations of earthquakes. Long after the ground stops shaking, the reverberations from earthquakes shudder through the Earth. Sensitive detectors pick them on the far side of the world. Just as you can hear the difference between metal and wood if you tap them with a spoon, so scientists can "hear" the Earth's interior from the pattern of earthquake waves (page 106).

### Could we ever visit the center of the Earth?

No one has ever managed to drill more than 7 miles (12km) down. Even at this depth, pressures are so great and rock so hot and soft that drill bores close up as fast as they are drilled. It seems unlikely then that anyone will ever get through the thin crust to the mantle, let alone down to the core.

### What's the mantle made of?

The mantle is made of rock, like the crust. But the most common minerals are minerals that are rare on the surface, like perivskovite and olivine.

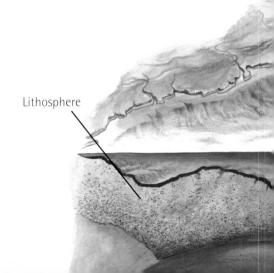

Lithosphere

## Where does the crust end?

The crust meets the mantle along a boundary called the Mohorovicic discontinuity. Chemically, this is a distinct break. But the top of the mantle is just as rigid as the crust. So scientists often group the top of the mantle together with the crust and call it the lithosphere. "Litho" means stone. Beneath the lithosphere is a layer that flows like very, very, sticky treacle called the asthenosphere.

▼ **Crack in the Earth**

*The Earth's surface is cracked in many places. One of the biggest cracks is under the middle of the oceans. Here the tectonic plates that form the Earth's rigid shell or lithosphere are pulling apart. As they do, molten rock from the mantle oozes up, cools, and solidifies, forming a long ridge of rock.*

## Are there any gaps in the crust?

Yes, the crust—or rather the lithosphere (see left)—is actually broken into 20 or so giant bits called tectonic plates. Molten material from the mantle oozes up along the cracks, creating volcanoes—especially where they are pulling apart.

## How hot is it in the Earth?

In the lithosphere, the temperature climbs 63°F (35°C) every 3,300 feet (1,000m) you go down. The core reaches 12,600°F (7,000°C).

Mantle

Molten rock oozes up between the plates

The solidified magma forms a mid-ocean ridge

# QUIZ

1 How thick is the Earth's mantle a) 186 miles (300km) b) 1,860 miles (3,000km) c) 18,600 miles (30,000 km)?

2 In 1864, the famous book 'Journey to the Center of the Earth' was written by a) Nathaniel Hawthorne b) Charles Dickens c) Jules Verne?

3 There are continents on the Earth's core: true or false?

4 Most of the water in the oceans came from inside the Earth: true or false?

5 What have the Earth beneath the crust and old cloaks in common?

6 Some caves reach right down into the mantle: true or false?

7 Which one is lightest (least dense): a) the Earth's crust b) its mantle c) its core?

8 The world's deepest borehole in the Kola Peninsula in Russia goes down: a) 2 miles (3km) b) 7 miles (12km) c) 50 miles (80km)?

Answers
1. b) 2. c) 3. True 4. True
5. Both are called mantles
6. False 7. a) 8. b)

101

# Mountain building

## What are the world's highest mountains?

THE WORLD'S HIGHEST MOUNTAINS are the Himalayan mountains in Asia to the north of India. Here are all the world's ten tallest mountains, including Mount Everest, the very highest mountain of all, 29,021 feet (8,848m) high. But each continent has its high mountain range. There are the Andes in South America where there are many peaks over 20,000 feet (6,100m), the Rocky Mountains in North America, and the Alps in Europe.

▲ The Himalayas
*The Himalayas include such soaring peaks as K2 (28,244 feet/8,611m), Kanchenjunga (28,201 feet/8,598m) and Lhotse (27,916 feet/8,511m) as well as Mt. Everest.*

▼ Folding mountains
*Whether they are made from sediments settling on the seabed or from volcanic plateaus, most rocks form in flat layers. But as the plates of the Earth's crust move together, folds form as the layers are squeezed horizontally.*

## Have mountains always been there?

New mountains are being created all the time—although it takes many millions of years. Most of the world's highest mountains were formed quite recently in Earth's history. The Himalayan mountains, for instance, have been built up within the last 40 million years—and they are still growing even today.

## How are mountains made?

Some mountains are created by volcanic eruptions, but most mountains are thrown up by the tremendous power of the Earth's crust moving. Some mountains are huge slabs called fault blocks or "horst" that are thrown up by powerful earthquakes. The biggest ranges, though, are created by the crumpling of rocks as the great plates that make up the Earth's crust squash together. Mountains that form like this are called fold mountains. The Alps, Himalayas, and the Andes are all fold mountains.

As plates of the Earth's crust push together, layers of rocks get pushed up in folds

If the plates go on pushing, the layers may overturn and snap

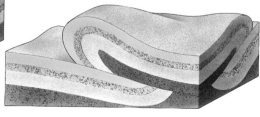

Eventually the layers may begin to snap altogether, creating a "nappe"

## Where do mountains form?

Fold mountains are usually thrown up where the edge of a continent is crumpled as it collides with another tectonic plate. The Andes, for example, were crumpled up right along the edge of South America, as the plate beneath the Pacific ocean crunched into it. When two continents collide, the mountains may be huge. The Himalayas are being thrown up where the Indian plate is driving into Asia.

▼ **Block mountains**
*The movement of tectonic plates can put rocks under such strain that they fracture, creating cracks called faults in the rock. Large faulted blocks of rock may then be thrown up to create mountains.*

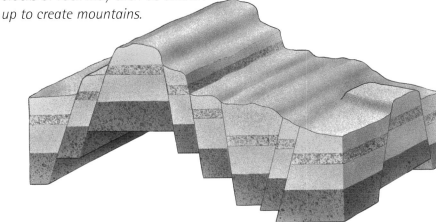

## Will mountains always be there?

No, each mountain range is slowly worn down by the weather, and by rivers and moving ice, over millions of years. Scotland's Caledonian mountains and North America's Appalachians were once among the world's highest, but are gradually being worn flat. Other parts of the world that are now completely flat were once mountainous.

## When did mountains form?

Fold mountains are usually created in fairly short mountain-building phases. By short, geologists mean a few tens of millions of years, rather than hundreds. In different parts of the world, geologists identify different phases from the past. In North America, there are phases called the Huronian, Nevadian, and Pasadenian. In Europe, there were the Caledonian, Hercynian, and Alpine. Most of today's major mountain ranges were formed in the last 50 million years.

## Why are some mountains snow-capped?

Air gets colder as you get higher. Above a certain level, called the snowline, it is always too cold for snow to melt, so it stays all year round. The snowline is 16,500 feet (5,000m) up in the tropics, 8,900 feet (2,710m) in the Alps, and at sea level at the Poles.

# QUIZ

1 What is the highest mountain in North America?

2 How high is the Vinson Massif in Antarctica:
a) 4,070 feet (1241m)
b) 11,683 feet (3,562m) c
) 16,859 feet (5,140m)?

3 Mt. Everest is gaining height: true or false?

4 The Black Forest in Germany was originally volcanoes: true or false?

5 Which continent has no mountains over 16,400 feet (5,000m)?

6 A syncline is a) a steep slope b) a downfold in rock c) a bad habit?

7 How did Japan's highest mountain form?

# Volcanic eruptions

## What are volcanoes?

**V**OLCANOES ARE PLACES where molten rock from the Earth's hot interior comes up through the ground. The molten rock is called magma, and sometimes it just oozes slowly onto the surface as a red hot stream called lava. Sometimes, though, the magma builds up underground then bursts through in a huge explosion called an eruption. When this happens, steam and ash are thrown high into the air, ash and hot cinders rain down far around, the volcano, and streams of lava gush from the neck of the volcano.

### ▲ Crater
*Around the top of a volcano's vent, there is usually a wide mouth called a crater. Occasionally, the entire top of the volcano collapses into the magma chamber to form a huge crater called a caldera.*

### ▼ Types of volcano
*No volcano is quite the same. Each has its own shape and way of erupting—and each eruption is slightly different. But there are three main kinds of volcano: shield volcanoes, cone volcanoes, and composite volcanoes.*

### How does the magma get out through the ground?
Before it emerges, magma builds up in a space underground called the magma chamber. The pressure of magma bubbling up underneath builds until it pushes magma up to the surface—either through a pipe called a vent, or a crack called a fissure.

### Are all volcanoes made of lava?
No, some are made of ash, and some are made of alternate layers of lava and ash.

### Are all volcanoes the same?
No. There are many different kinds. The kind of volcano depends mainly on the nature of the magma. When magma is low in silica, it is very runny. It gushes out from cracks in the ground and flows out over wide areas and hardens to form what are called shield volcanoes, because they are shaped like shields. When magma is high in silica, it piles up around the vent. A tall cone is built up in successive eruptions. It is these cones which make the most distinctive volcanoes, like Mt. Fuji in Japan, and Kilimanjaro in Kenya.

Shield volcanoes are formed by gentle eruptions of runny lava

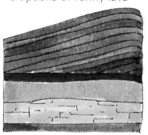

Cone volcanoes are built up by successive eruptions of sticky, acidic lava

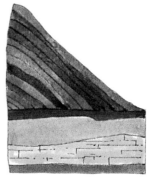

► **Lava stream**
*The red hot stream of molten rock called lava looks frightening, but it is rarely lava that kills people in a volcano eruption. The real killers are usually the clouds of choking ash that bury the landscape far around—or worse still, high-speed flows of mud or glowing ash called nuée ardenté.*

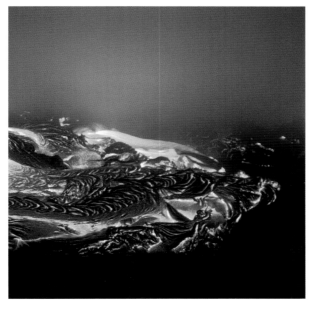

# QUIZ

1. Which is the tallest volcano in Japan?
2. What volcano erupted and buried the Ancient Roman town of Pompeii in Italy a) Etna b) Stromboli c) Vesuvius?
3. Edinburgh Castle is built on an extinct volcano: true or false?
4. Most of the world's active volcanoes are on land: true or false?
5. Can volcanoes change the world's weather?
6. Vulcanologists try to predict eruptions by looking for a slight swelling in a volcano: true or false?

## Where are volcanoes found?

Volcanos are found mainly along the boundaries between the great tectonic plates that make up the Earth's surface—and in particular, a ring around the Pacific Ocean called the Ring of Fire. They are also found on "hot spots"—places where columns of hot rock bubble up under the crust and burn through.

## What is a dormant volcano?

Some active volcanoes erupt almost continuously, but others go quiet for periods and so are said to be dormant. If they never erupt, they are extinct.

## Why do some volcanoes erupt explosively?

When the magma is very thick and sticky, it can clog up a volcano's vent. When it finally bursts through, it is like popping the cork of a champagne bottle. Steam and carbon dioxide gas dissolved under pressure in the magma boil and bubble violently as the pressure is released, and these bubbles drive the magma in an explosive froth up through the vent. The old clog is shattered to smithereens by the explosion, forming ash, and cinder that are hurled for miles around the volcano.

Composite volcanoes are built up from alternate layers of lava and ash

In each eruption the ash falls slowly to settle on top of the lava flow

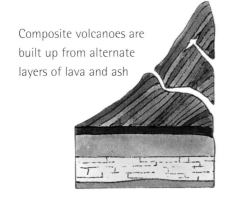

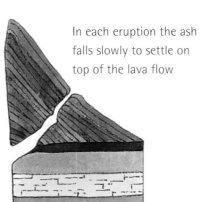

# Earthquakes

## What are earthquakes?

EARTHQUAKES ARE A SHAKING of the ground. Some are so slight they can barely rock a cradle. But some are so violent they can shake down mountains and destroy cities. All kinds of things can set off small earthquakes, from the rumbling of heavy traffic to the eruption of a volcano. But the biggest earthquakes are set off by the shuddering of the vast tectonic plates that make up the Earth's surface as they grind slowly together underground.

### What sets off an earthquake?

Tectonic plates are sliding past each other all the time but sometimes they jam. Then the rock bends and stretches for a while until the strain gets so much that it snaps and the plates lurch on again. The snapping of the rock and sudden jolting of the plates sends shock waves out in all directions. When these waves reach the surface, they create earthquakes.

### Where do earthquakes start?

The starting point of an earthquake underground is called the hypocenter or focus. The epicentre is the point on the surface above the hypocenter. Earthquakes are strongest at the epicenter, and get gradually weaker farther away.

The Earth in cross-section: P waves

Crust

P waves are waves that alternately stretch and squeeze the rock

Mantle

Outer core

P waves are refracted as they pass through the Earth's liquid core

Inner core

S waves are waves that move the ground from side to side or up and down

▶ P and S waves
*Earthquake body waves can travel right through the world. Some, called P waves, can reach the other side in barely an hour and register on seismometers far from the earthquake. S waves take only a little longer. Comparing readouts from two or three stations pinpoints the earthquake's epicentre. The way the different kinds of waves are refracted or bent through the Earth reveals a great deal about its interior.*

S waves are deflected altogether by the liquid core

The Earth in cross-section: S waves

106

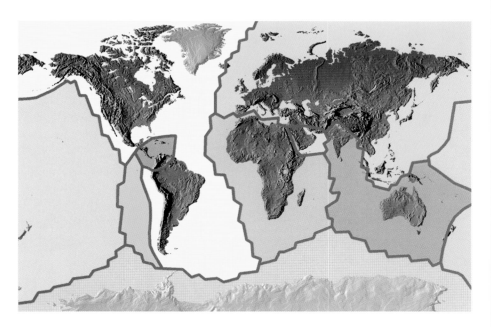

▲ **Earthquake zones**
*Earthquakes tend to occur mostly along the boundaries of tectonic plates. Places like Japan and Mexico are particularly prone to quakes.*

## What are earthquake zones?

Earthquake zones are places particularly prone to earthquakes. Most of these lie on or near the edges of tectonic plates. Many major cities, such as Los Angeles, Tokyo, and Mexico City, lie in earthquake zones.

## How long do earthquakes last?

Most earthquakes are over quickly, lasting less than a minute. The longest, which hit Alaska in March 1964, lasted just four minutes.

## How are quakes measured?

With a device called a seismometer, which responds to vibrations and records them on a computer display.

## What are earthquake waves?

Earthquake or "seismic" waves are the vibrations from earthquakes. There are two main kinds. Body waves travel underground at huge speeds, and can vibrate all around the world. Surface waves travel out along the surface from the epicenter and are much slower, but it is these which do the real damage in an earthquake. Surface waves called Q waves shake the ground from side to side, bringing down tall buildings. Surface waves called Rayleigh waves shake the ground up and down, and seem to roll through sandy or muddy ground like waves in the sea.

## What is the Richter scale?

The Richter scale shows an earthquake's magnitude—that is, how strong the waves are on a seismometer. Each point indicates a tenfold increase in size. A really big earthquake is at least 6 on the Richter scale.

# QUIZ

1 Which Japanese city was devastated by an earthquake in 1995:
a) Kobe b) Nagasaki
c) Tokyo?

2 What is the name of the fault that sets off earthquakes in California?

3 Which year was San Francisco burned to the ground after an earthquake: a) 1854
b) 1906 c) 1937?

4 Giant waves called tsunami are set off by
a) tidal movements
b) volcanoes c) undersea earthquakes?

5 The ancient Chinese detected earthquakes with brass frogs: true or false?

6 Earthquakes can make rock rise and fall like tides in the sea: true or false?

Answers
1. a)   2. San Andreas  3. b)
4. b) and c)  5. True
6. False

# Weathering

## How do hills wear down?

**H**ILLS AND MOUNTAINS are all worn flat eventually. It takes many thousands or even millions of years, but the combined attack of the weather, chemicals in rainwater, running water, wind, glaciers and various other "agents of erosion" will wear them flatter and flatter. Valleys will get broader, hilltops will get lower, ridges will get narrower until at last an entire mountain range is turned into a lowland plain.

▲ Grand Canyon.
*The Grand Canyon was carved by the Colorado river as it cut down through the Colorado Plateau, which was lifted up thousands of feet in a massive movement of the Earth's crust.*

### What is weathering?
Although rock is hard, the assault of the weather will turn even the hardest granite into soft clay over time. The weather breaks down rocks through the attack of moisture, heat and cold and chemicals in rainwater. Usually only rocks near the surface are affected, but water trickling down through the ground can weather rocks far underground. The more extreme the climate, the faster rock weathers.

### How does frost break rock?
When water freezes it expands by almost a tenth. So when it freezes inside cracks, it can push them apart. This expansion can exert a pressure of 6,600 pounds (3,000kg) on an area of rock the size of a postage stamp. As water freezes and thaws repeatedly inside cracks, this pressure can shatter rocks.

### What is scree?
Scree is the huge piles of angular rock you often see littering mountain slopes. As the rock shatters, the chunks fall off and build up at the bottom of the slope.

Limestone scenery

### What is karst?
Streams and rainwater absorb carbon dioxide gas from the soil and air, and so become a weak acid called carbonic acid. Most things are unaffected by this acidity, but limestone is very easily corroded by this acid. So when limestone is near the surface, water trickling down through the rock can dissolve huge holes in it. This can create a spectacular landscape of gorges, caves and jagged rock called karst, after the Karst region of Bosnia.

◀ Uluru
*Uluru or Ayers Rock is a dome of sandstone in the middle of the Australian bush. Deep furrows down its side testify to the erosive power of running water even in this dry place.*

▲ **Wave rock**
*This fantastically curved rock was carved by floods of water in much wetter times. A dry climate has preserved its shape since.*

## What is exfoliation?

In dry areas, rocks often flake off in leaves at the surface. This is called exfoliation. It was once thought this was due to extremes of heat and cold. Now scientists think it is caused by the growth of salt crystals in water that seeps into the rock.

## What are tors?

Tors are outcrops of rock often seen on the tops of hills on granite moors, such as Dartmoor in England. The tor began as bedrock beneath a hilltop, but as water trickled into cracks, it rotted away below the ground—except where there were massive block with few cracks. These massive blocks were left standing out above the ground as the rotted rock around was worn away.

## What happens to weathered rock?

Fragments of weathered rock roll downslope to be washed away by rivers, creep down slowly, or get gradually worn finer and form the basis for soil.

◄ **Shattered peak**
*Thousands of years of frost have shattered the peaks of high mountains like the Matterhorn, creating sharp, craggy, broken ridges and a jagged rock summit.*

# QUIZ

1 In China there is a spectacular range of pointed limestone hills made of eroded limestone. What are they called?

2 The corroded grooves in limestone are a) tongue and groove b) brett and pull c) clint and gryke?

3 The flaking of rock on the Yosemite dome in California is caused by the removal of the weight of rock above: true or false?

4 Rabbits make rock vulnerable to erosion by their burrowing: true or false?

5 What's the main erosive force on mountaintops?

**Answers**
1. Guilin Hills
2. c) 3. True 4. True
5. Frost shattering

# Rivers

## What makes rivers run?

RIVERS ARE KEPT RUNNING BY RAINFALL. The rain does not always run off the land directly into rivers. Sometimes it sinks into the ground on hilltops and emerges lower down through holes called springs. Sometimes it is frozen into ice and snow for a while and does not reach the river until it melts. But without rain every river will stop running eventually. The more it rains, the fuller the river will be. Floods usually occur a little while after heavy rainstorms, or after winter snows melt in spring.

High in the hills, a small stream tumbles over rocks in a narrow V-shaped valley

Farther downstream rivers flow in smooth channels made of their own deposited material.

Oxbow lake formed by a cut-off meander

Toward the sea, the river may flow across the broad plains of silt it has washed down

As tributaries join, the river grows bigger

▶ **Changing river**
*Near its start, high in the hills, streams simply tumble this way and that over rocks in steep valleys. But as they become broad rivers farther down, they begin to flow in smooth channels made entirely of fine material worn away higher up and washed down by the river.*

Lower down, the river may wind across the valley floor in broad meanders

110

## Why do rivers wind?

All rivers tend to wind, especially as they near the sea, where they often wind in horseshoe shape bends called meanders. The biggest meanders occur where the river flows wide and smooth through soft muddy banks. They form partly because of the way water in the river spirals, and partly because of the way the river wears away its bed and banks in some places, and deposits grains of mud and sand in others.

## Where do rivers start and end?

Rivers start off as small streams high in the hills. As they flow downhill, they are joined by other streams, called tributaries. They grow bigger and bigger, and at last flow into a sea or lake.

## How do rivers shape the land?

Over many thousands of years, rivers can wear away the land. First, they carve downwards to create deep V-shaped valleys. Then they swing sideways to widen the valleys, eventually, into broad plains. They may also bury the valley floor or plain in fine silt.

As it nears the sea and slows down, the river may drop its sediment load and split into branches

## What is a waterfall?

A waterfall is a place where a river plunges straight over a ledge of rock. Typically, they occur where the river flows across a band of hard rock. The river wears away the soft material, leaving the hard rock barely touched. The highest waterfall is the Angel Falls in Venezuela, which plunges 3,211 feet (979m).

## What is a delta?

Deltas are areas of sediment—sand, silt, and mud—piled up in a river's mouth, as the river hits the sea, or a lake, and slows down. Often the river splits up into many smaller branches called distributaries.

## How do rivers move silt and sand?

Rivers carry their "load" of sediment in three ways. Big stones are rolled along the riverbed. Smaller grains are bounced along the bed. The finest grains float in the water.

## What is an oxbow lake?

An oxbow lake is a small lake formed where a river meander has been cut off. The river wears away the outside bend of the meander, making its neck narrower and narrower, until the river cuts through, cutting off the meander.

# QUIZ

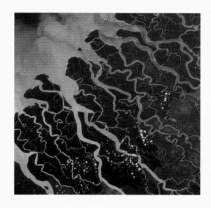

1 The Mississippi River forms a delta as it enters the Gulf of Mexico: true or false?

2 River flow reaches its peak a) just before a rain storm b) during a rain storm c) just after a rainstorm?

3 What is the world's longest river?

4 Is river braiding a) where rivers branch b) where rivers wear their banks away c) raised river banks?

5 The River Orinoco, a tributary of the Amazon, flows uphill: true or false?

# Glaciers

## What are glaciers?

**G**LACIERS ARE RIVERS OF SLOWLY moving ice that form when it is too cold for snow to melt. Nowadays, they form only in high mountains and towards the North and South Poles. But in the past, during cold periods called Ice Ages, glaciers were far more widespread. Huge areas of North America and Europe were under ice, and the ice left dramatic marks on the landscape.

## How do glaciers form

Glaciers form when new snow, which scientists call névé, falls on top of old snow. The weight of the new snow compacts the old snow into denser snow, which the scientists call firn. In firn, all the air is squeezed out, so it looks less like fluffy snow and more like white ice. Over time, the ice is compacted more and more until it turns into thick white glacier ice and begins to flow, very slowly, downhill.

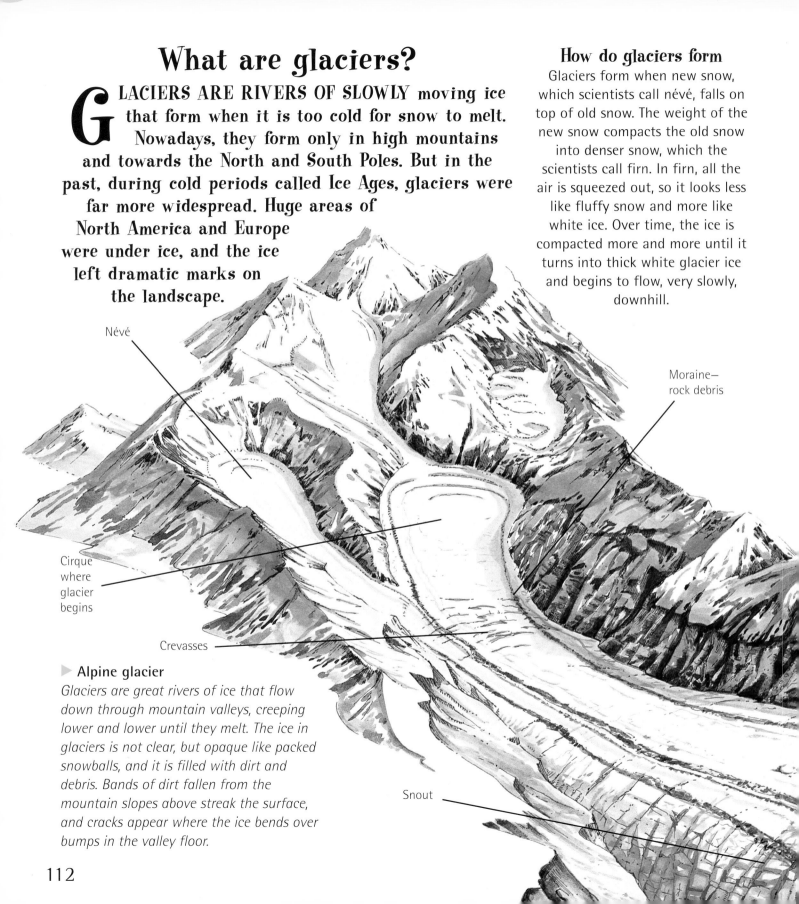

Névé

Moraine— rock debris

Cirque where glacier begins

Crevasses

Snout

▶ **Alpine glacier**

*Glaciers are great rivers of ice that flow down through mountain valleys, creeping lower and lower until they melt. The ice in glaciers is not clear, but opaque like packed snowballs, and it is filled with dirt and debris. Bands of dirt fallen from the mountain slopes above streak the surface, and cracks appear where the ice bends over bumps in the valley floor.*

## How do glaciers shape the land?

Glaciers move very slowly but their sheer weight and size gives them enormous power to carve out the landscape. They carve out huge U-shaped valleys, gouge out great bowls in hills called cirques, and truncate (slice away) entire hills and valleys. They can also move huge amounts of rock debris then drop it in large distinctive piles called moraine.

## Do glaciers ever melt?

Yes, they are melting all the time. As they flow downhill into warmer air, the end, or "snout" of the glacier melts. But snow falling up in the mountains replenishes the top of the glacier and keeps it from shrinking—unless the climate begins to warm.

## What are fjords?

Fjords are very deep inlets in the coasts of Norway, New Zealand, and Canada. They were carved out by glaciers in the last Ice Age, then flooded by the sea.

▲ **Icebergs**

*Icebergs are large floating chunks of ice that break off the end of ice sheets, icecaps, and glaciers and float out to sea.*

## When was the Ice Age?

There is not just one Ice Age. There have been four in the last billion years, and each of these has many colder periods called glacials and warmer ones called interglacials. There have been 17 glacials in the last 1.6 million years, and the last ended just 10,000 years ago.

## Why do Ice Ages happen?

They are probably caused by regular wobbles of the Earth's axis, called Milankovitch cycles.

# QUIZ

1  Where is the world's longest glacier?

2  Glaciers take how long to flow 6 feet (1.8m) a) a year b) a day c) a second?

3  What did the ship *Titanic* hit before it sank?

4  The largest iceberg ever was almost as big as Denmark: true or false?

5  In 1913 an iceberg was seen floating past the Statue of Liberty: true or false?

6  The landscape of Cape Cod in Massachusetts was shaped by ice: true or false?

7  What continent has the biggest area of ice?

8  What are the cracks in glaciers called?

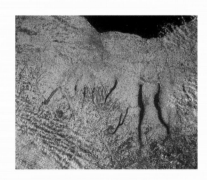

**Answers**
1. Antarctica 2. b) 3. An iceberg 4. True 5. False 6. True 7. Antarctica 8. Crevasses

# Deserts

## What are deserts?

**D**ESERTS ARE VERY DRY PLACES where it hardly ever rains. Some deserts are very hot, like the Sahara desert in northern Africa. Some are very cold, like Antarctica. In hot deserts, what little rain there is quickly evaporates, so there is little water available for plants. So plants are very scarce in the desert. Indeed, most deserts are bare rock, rubble, or sand, with no soil.

▼ **Desert landforms**

*The bare, dry landscape of the desert has its own distinctive range of landforms. With no water to round hills, the landscape is jagged, and filled with odd-shaped rocks sculpted by the wind, as well as seas of sand dunes.*

**Key:**
1. *Mushroom rock*
2. *Sand dunes*
3. *Sand ripples*
4. *Deflation hollow (blown out by wind)*
5. *Oasis*

### Where do deserts occur?

Many deserts occur in the subtropics—that is, just outside the tropics. The natural circulation of air around the world means air is very calm, clear and dry. The Sahara and the Great Australian desert are subtropical deserts. Some deserts, like Chile's Atacama, occur in the lee of mountain ranges that act as a barrier to rain-bearing winds. A few deserts are near seacoasts and are dry because cool ocean currents dry the air.

### How hot are deserts?

Hot deserts can be the hottest places in the world, because there is no moisture in the air to block the sun's rays. Summer temperatures in the Sudan desert in Africa can soar to 133°F (56°C), hotter than anywhere else in the world. But even here it can get cold at night, because the heat escapes through the clear skies.

### Are all deserts sandy?

No. Deserts that are vast seas of sand are actually quite rare. Just as many deserts are pebbly or rocky.

### Are there any rivers in the desert?

Some rivers, like Egypt's River Nile, start in wet regions outside the desert and flow right through it and out the other side. Others flow only when it rains, leaving a dry riverbed most of the year round. Rivers like these are called ephemeral.

## Mushroom rock

## Barchan

Wind

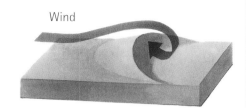

▲ **Wind action**

*Wind plays an important part in shaping the desert landscape. Wind bouncing sand along the ground can undercut rocks to create distinctive mushroom-shaped rocks.*

### What is a wadi?

A wadi is a gorge cut by rivers in the desert when it rains. Most of the time it is completely dry, but after a rain storm it can fill suddenly with water in a flash flood.

### How is the desert landscape shaped?

Since desert sand is very dry, it is easily blown up by the wind, and the desert has its own range of landforms sculpted from sand hurled by the wind. The high temperatures mean that rocks can easily be corroded by salts as well— or even baked to breaking point.

### What is a sand dune?

A dune is sand blown into a mound by the wind. Dunes come in many different shapes and sizes, including stars, long ridges (called seifs) and crescents (barchans). It all depends on how sandy it is, and where the wind blows from.

Barchans are moved along gradually as sand is blown up one side and rolls down the other.

# QUIZ

1 How much of the world's land surface is covered by desert: a) a tenth b) a fifth c) one half?

2 What is the world's biggest desert?

3 Vast areas of central Asia and China are covered in a thick layer of yellow dust: true or false?

4 What is an oasis?

5 Buttes are a) sheer-sided rocks b) deep dry gorges c) the end of a valley?

6 The technical name for wind action is a) alluvial b) aeolian c) ventilation?

7 Where is Uluru, or Ayers Rock?

8 There used to be snow in the Sahara desert: true or false?

**Answers**
1. b)   2. The Sahara in Africa
3. True; the dust called loess was blown by winds in the Ice Age
4. A moist area in the desert
5. a)   6. b)   7. Australia   8. True

# Coasts

## How do waves shape coasts?

ON EXPOSED COASTS, the pounding of waves can wear away solid rock, undercutting hills to create sheer cliffs. As the cliffs are worn back farther, they leave behind a wide ledge of rock at sea level called a wavecut platform, or upstanding remnants of the cliff called stacks. On sheltered coasts, however, waves can build up the coast, washing in sand to create beaches.

### Where does sand come from?

Sand is what is left after material broken off cliffs and rocky coasts has been battered this way and that in the sea for many years.

### What is shingle?

Shingle is like sand, but with much bigger grains, the size of small peas, rather than sugar. Water sorts different grades of grain out, so that some beaches are pebbly, some are shingly, some are sandy.

▼ **Coastal landforms**

*Constant battering by waves and sea water gives coasts their own range of landforms. In exposed places such as headlands, the coast is rocky, with steep cliffs, wavecut rock platforms, stacks, and even natural rock arches. In sheltered places, sand worn away from the headlands piles up as beaches.*

Sand piles up as beaches in bays

Waves wear exposed headlands into cliffs and stacks

**▲ Blowhole**

*Sometimes, the sheer pressure of water from a breaking wave may force water up through a crack to burst through the top of a cliff like a fountain. This is called a blowhole.*

**▲ Rock arch**

*As waves wear away the base of a cliff over the years, they may eventually wear right through a headland, creating a natural rock arch, if the rock higher up stays intact.*

**▲ Stack**

*As the waves go on wearing away at the base of the cliff, the rock arch gets wider and eventually is so weak that it collapses, leaving just a column called a stack.*

In places on low coasts, salty lagoons form

## How are waves made?

Waves begin as wind blowing across the open sea whips the surface into ripples. If the wind is strong enough and blows far enough over the water, the ripples build into waves. The stronger the wind and the farther it blows (called the fetch), the bigger the waves are. In big oceans like the Atlantic and Pacific, the fetch is so big that huge "swells" build up.

## How do waves move?

Waves move like a relay race. The water in them barely moves, but simply goes round in a circle, like the roller on a conveyor belt.

## What are tides?

Tides are the slight rising and falling of the sea—usually twice a day—as the Earth turns round. They are caused by the pull of the Moon's gravity on the waters of the oceans.

## Why do waves break?

Waves break when the water becomes so shallow that the water cannot complete a circle. Instead, water rolling round the top of the wave spills forward onto the beach, then falls back.

# QUIZ

1. Groynes on a beach are a) barriers of rock b) sand bars c) fences put up to to stop sand being washed along the beach?

2. What is a bight?

3. Sand moves along a beach when waves hit the beach at an angle: true or false?

4. A coast with lots of islands and inlets is called a) an archipelago b) an insular coast c) an escarpment?

5. What is an ebb tide?

6. Spring tides are a) tides that happen only in spring b) tides that race up and down c) the most extreme tides each month?

7. What is a long, narrow continental size inlet?

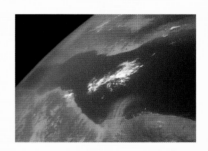

Answers

1. c)   2. A very large bay
3. True; this is called longshore drift   4. a)   5. A falling tide
6. c)   7. A gulf

# Caves

## What are caves?

CAVES ARE LARGE NATURAL HOLES UNDERGROUND. Some are little bigger than a closet. Others are bigger than a cathedral. The biggest caves are called caverns. Some are single caves. Others are huge networks of chambers linked by long passageways through the rock.

▲ **Stalagmites and stalactites**
*Hanging needles and pillars formed by dripping water can turn limestone caverns into natural cathedrals.*

### What is a pothole?

Because limestone rock has so many cracks or joints, most streams quickly disappear into the ground. The hole down which a stream runs into the ground is called a swallowhole. Over time, mild acids dissolved in the water may corrode the crack in the rock into a deep vertical shaft. This is a pothole. Sometimes streams plunge into them as spectacular waterfalls.

### How do caves form?

Caves form in many ways. Some are the old pipes that lava flowed through in volcanoes. Some are created when earthquakes crack the rock. Some are opened up by the sea. But the biggest and most extensive caves are usually in limestone. Streams and rainwater absorb carbon dioxide gas from the soil and air, turning it into a weak acid. Limestone has plenty of cracks called joints. As the acid water trickles down through these joints into limestone, it gradually dissolves away the rock underground. As more and more of the rock around a joint is dissolved away, it forms a cavern.

▶ **Limestone underground**
*Slightly acidic water trickling down through cracks in limestone gradually eats away the rock underground, opening up caverns and potholes. Below a certain level, called the water table, the rock is completely saturated with water, and the caverns are flooded.*

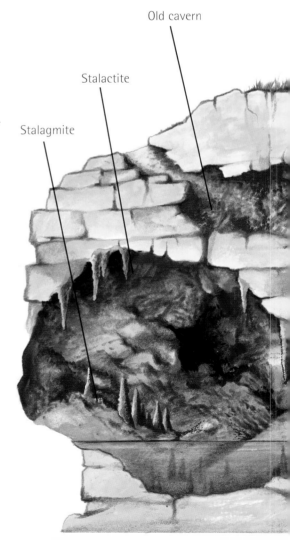

Old cavern

Stalactite

Stalagmite

## What are stalagmites and stalactites?

Stalagmites and stalactites are formations made by water dripping through the ceiling of a limestone cavern. Calcium carbonate dissolved in the water forms long, icicle-shaped deposits that hang from the ceiling. These are called stalactites. As water drips from a stalactite onto the cavern floor, calcium carbonate is also deposited on the floor, piling up in a narrow pinnacle called a stalagmite. Eventually, the stalagmite and stalactite may actually meet to form a pillar from floor to ceiling.

## Do caves last forever?

No. Although some are very old, most are gradually corroded away. As more and more of the roof rots away, it gets weaker and may eventually collapse, leaving just a large hole in the ground, called a polje. If an entire interlinked string of caverns collapses, it may create a long cliff-walled valley called a gorge, though gorges may also form in other ways.

## What are gallery caves?

Gallery caves are long, dry tunnel-like caves originally formed by an underground stream, but left dry when the water table (the level of water) in the rock dropped.

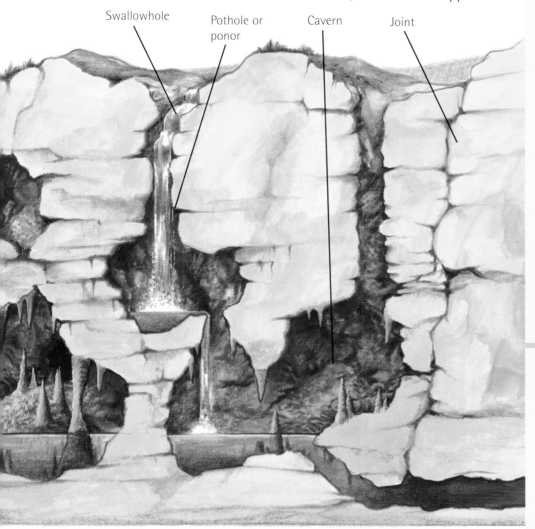

Swallowhole    Pothole or ponor    Cavern    Joint

1 The world's longest cave network is Mammoth Cave in Kentucky. It is a) 12 miles (20km) long b) 120 miles (200km) long c) 350 miles (560km) long?

2 The world's biggest single cave is the Sarawak Chamber in Sarawak. It is big enough to hold a) a house b) the Louisiana Superdome c) the city of New York?

3 What is the technical name for an expert on caves?

4 There are huge caves under the ocean, created by waves: true or false?

5 Stalagmites and stalactites are covered in material that makes them shine in the dark: true or false?

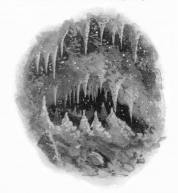

Answers
1. c)  2. b)  3. A speleologist
4. False  5. True

Why does the
Moon shine?

How hot is the Sun?

How many stars
are there in the
sky?

Who were the first
men on the Moon?

How do rockets
work in space?

How do satellites
stay up?

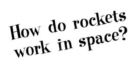

Is there life on
Mars?

120

Why do stars twinkle?

How did the Universe begin?

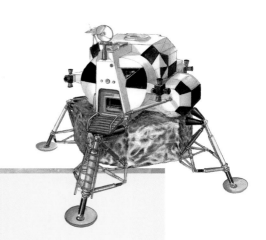

# Space

Why is Venus pink?

# The Earth

## What is the Earth?

THE EARTH IS ONE OF THE NINE PLANETS that continually circle the Sun, making up the solar system. It is the third planet out from the Sun, between Venus and Mars, and like them and Mercury, the planet nearest the Sun, it is a ball made largely of rock. What makes it special is the fact that its surface is two thirds covered by water. It is also the only planet with oxygen in its atmosphere. Without water and oxygen, there would be no life.

## How was the Earth formed?

No one is absolutely sure how the Earth began. But most astronomers think that about five billion years ago there was just a vast cloud of hot gas and dust circling around the newly formed Sun. Then gradually, parts of this cloud began to clump together, pulled together by gravity. These clumps grew to form the planets.

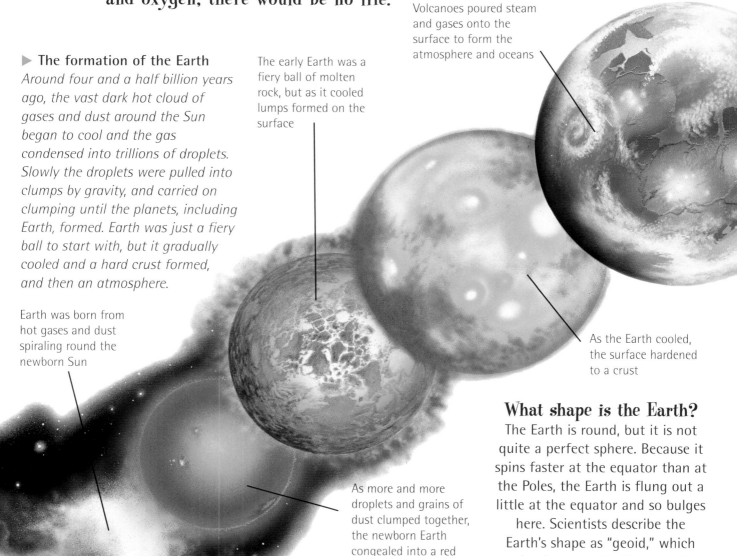

► **The formation of the Earth**
*Around four and a half billion years ago, the vast dark hot cloud of gases and dust around the Sun began to cool and the gas condensed into trillions of droplets. Slowly the droplets were pulled into clumps by gravity, and carried on clumping until the planets, including Earth, formed. Earth was just a fiery ball to start with, but it gradually cooled and a hard crust formed, and then an atmosphere.*

The early Earth was a fiery ball of molten rock, but as it cooled lumps formed on the surface

Volcanoes poured steam and gases onto the surface to form the atmosphere and oceans

Earth was born from hot gases and dust spiraling round the newborn Sun

As more and more droplets and grains of dust clumped together, the newborn Earth congealed into a red hot ball

As the Earth cooled, the surface hardened to a crust

## What shape is the Earth?

The Earth is round, but it is not quite a perfect sphere. Because it spins faster at the equator than at the Poles, the Earth is flung out a little at the equator and so bulges here. Scientists describe the Earth's shape as "geoid," which simply means Earth-shaped.

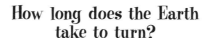

## How far is Earth from the Sun?

About 93 million miles (150 million km) on average, but it varies according to the time of year. Its closest, on January 3, is called the perihelion. The farthest point, on July 4, is called the aphelion.

The crust cooled to form continents

## How long does the Earth take to turn?

The Earth turns around in 24 hours, which is why days are 24 hours long. Actually, it takes 23 hours, 56 minutes and 4.09 seconds to turn around, but because the Earth moves round the Sun as well as turning, it takes exactly 24 hours for the Sun to return to the same place in the sky.

## Why do we have leap years?

It takes the Earth just over 365 days to go round, which is why a year is 365 days. The journey actually takes 365.242 days, not 365. To make up for the 0.242 days and keep the calendar in step with the Earth, we add an extra day to February every fourth year, the leap year. Even this doesn't make it quite right, so a leap year is left out at the end of three centuries out of four.

## Does the Earth tilt over?

Yes. It spins round on a line between the Poles called its axis. The axis is tilted over at 23.5° in relation to the Sun.

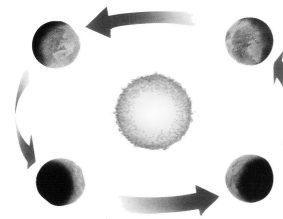

◀ Seasons

*We get seasons because the Earth is always tilted over in the same direction. So when the Earth is on one side of the Sun, the northern hemisphere (the world north of the equator) is tilted toward the Sun, bringing summer here. When the Earth is on the other side of the Sun, the northern hemisphere is tilted away, bringing winter. The seasons are reversed in the south.*

# QUIZ

1  How old is the Earth:
  a) 46,000 years
  b) 4.6 million years
  c) 4.6 billion years?

2  It is shorter to go from pole to pole then back than to go around the equator: true or false?

3  The astronomer who first realized Earth goes round the Sun was a) Ptolemy b) Copernicus c) Hubble?

4  The Earth is moving round the Sun at 50,000 mph (80,000km/h): true or false?

5  The Earth is spinning at over 25,000 mph (40,000km/hour): true or false?

Answers
1. c)  2. False  3. b) Nicolaus Copernicus (1473-1543)
4. True  5. False; it takes 24 hours to spin 25,000 miles (40,000km)

# The Moon

## What is the Moon?

THE MOON IS A BALL OF ROCK, about a quarter of the size of the Earth. The Moon is held close to the Earth, like a ball on a string, by the mutual pull of the Moon and Earth's gravity. It circles continually around the Earth, taking about a month to go round, and as it goes round it also turns slowly on its axis, taking exactly the same time to go round—nearly 30 times slower than the Earth, which spins round in 24 hours.

◀ **Inside the Moon**
*The Moon has a very thick crust of solid rock (about 90 miles/150km thick), a very cool mantle of softer rock beneath, and a tiny metal core.*

### Why does the Moon shine?
The Moon is by far the brightest thing in the night sky. Indeed, it is so bright that you can often see it in the sky during the day too. But it does not have any light of its own. Moonlight is simply the Sun's light reflected off the white dust on the Moon's surface.

### What are the Moon's seas?
The large dark patches on the Moon that look like seas are, in fact, ancient lava flows from volcanoes.

▼ **Changing Moon**
*As the Moon circles the Earth over the course of a month, we see different amounts of its bright, sunlit side, so it appears to change shape. The changes are called the phases of the Moon. The phases are, from left to right: New Moon, Half Moon, Gibbous Moon, Full Moon, Gibbous Moon, Half Moon, Old Moon. When it is growing bigger it is said to be waxing; when it is growing smaller it is said to be waning.*

# QUIZ

▶ **Solar circle**
*When the Moon swings in between the Sun and the Earth, it blocks off the Sun from a small region on Earth for a few minutes. This is a solar eclipse.*

## Why does the Moon change shape?

It doesn't, but looks as if it does because as it circles the Earth we see its bright sunny side from different angles. At New Moon, it is between the Sun and the Earth, and we catch just a crescent-shaped glimpse of its bright side. Over the first two weeks, we see more and more of its bright side until at Full Moon, we see all of it. Over the next two weeks, we see less and less until we get back to a sliver, the Old Moon.

## How long is a month?

It takes the Moon 27.3 days to circle the Earth, but 29.53 days from one Full Moon to the next, because the Earth moves as well. This 29.53 day cycle is a lunar month. Calendar months are entirely artificial.

## What is an eclipse?

As the Moon goes round the Earth, it sometimes passes right into Earth's shadow, where the Sun's light is blocked off. This is called a lunar eclipse. Sometimes, the Moon passes between the Sun and the Earth and blocks off the Sun's light from a bit of the Earth. This is called a solar eclipse.

## Who were the first men on the Moon?

The first men on the Moon were Neil Armstrong and Buzz Aldrin of the US Apollo 11 mission. The Apollo's lunar module landed Armstrong and Aldrin on the Moon on the July 21, 1969.

1 Why does the Moon look the same size as the Sun?
2 Why does the Moon look like cheese?
3 There is water on the Moon: true or false?
4 A harvest moon is a) a golden moon b) a kind of cheese c) the bright full moon of harvest time?
5 The footprints left by the astronauts on the Moon in the 1960s are still there: true or false?
6 The terminator is a) Arnold Schwarzenegger b) the boundary between the Moon's dark and bright sides c) The dark side of the Moon?

**Answers**
1. Because the Moon is much, much nearer. 2. Because its surface is pitted with craters 3. True 4. c) 5. True 6. a) and b)!

# The Sun

## What is the Sun?

THE SUN IS A STAR, just like all the others you see in the night sky. The only difference is that it is just 93 million miles (150 million km) away, not many billions. It formed about 5 billion years ago after an earlier, much bigger star blew up, and now, in middle age, burns yellow and fairly steadily, giving the Earth daylight at remarkably constant temperatures. It will probably burn for another five billion years before burning out.

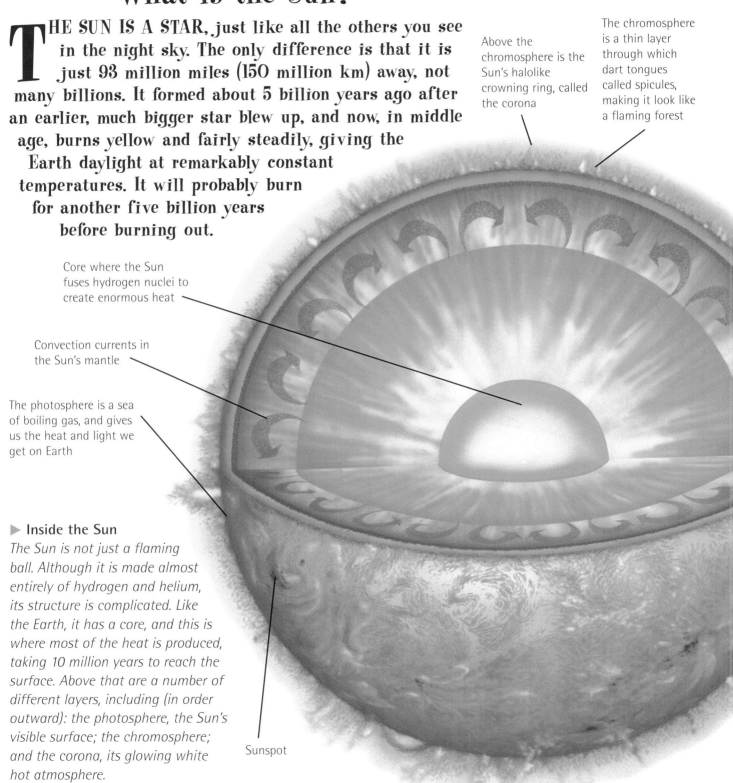

Above the chromosphere is the Sun's halolike crowning ring, called the corona

The chromosphere is a thin layer through which dart tongues called spicules, making it look like a flaming forest

Core where the Sun fuses hydrogen nuclei to create enormous heat

Convection currents in the Sun's mantle

The photosphere is a sea of boiling gas, and gives us the heat and light we get on Earth

Sunspot

▶ **Inside the Sun**
*The Sun is not just a flaming ball. Although it is made almost entirely of hydrogen and helium, its structure is complicated. Like the Earth, it has a core, and this is where most of the heat is produced, taking 10 million years to reach the surface. Above that are a number of different layers, including (in order outward): the photosphere, the Sun's visible surface; the chromosphere; and the corona, its glowing white hot atmosphere.*

126

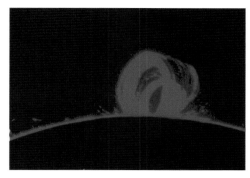

**▲ Solar prominences**
*Solar prominences are giant flame-like tongues of hot hydrogen that loop well over 100,000km out into space – as far as the Moon from the Earth.*

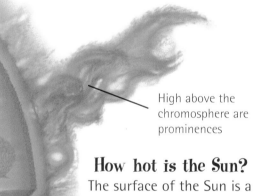

High above the chromosphere are prominences

## How hot is the Sun?
The surface of the Sun is a phenomenal 10,800°F (6,000°C). But its core is much, much hotter, at over 27 million°F (16 million°C)!

## Why is the Sun hot?
The Sun gets its heat because pressures deep in its core are enormous. Pressures are so great that the nuclei (centres) of hydrogen atoms are fused together as helium atoms. This nuclear fusion reaction—the same reaction that makes atomic bombs explode—releases a huge amount of heat.

## How big is the Sun?
The Sun is medium-sized for a star, but it is more than 170 times as big as the Earth. It is 863,000 miles (1,392,000km) across.

## What is the solar wind?
The solar wind is the stream of radioactive particles that is blowing out from the Sun all the time at hundreds of miles a second. These particles are so dangerous that life on Earth would be destroyed if the Earth were not protected from the wind by its magnetic field. A little of the wind creeps in through the clefts above the Poles, creating the light displays in the sky known as aurorae.

## What are sunspots?
Sunspots are dark blotches that can be seen on the Sun's surface with special instruments. They are dark because they are about 3,600°F (2,000°C) cooler than the rest of the the surface. They usually appear in groups and move across the Sun's face as it rotates— in about 37 days at the equator and 26 days nearer the Poles. The average number varies, reaching a maximum every 11 years, and may be linked to storm spells on Earth.

## What are solar flares?
Flares are eruptions from the Sun's surface that spout into space every now and then. They last about five minutes but they have the energy of one million atom bombs.

# QUIZ

1  A postage stamp size area of the Sun's surface shines with the power of a) 1000 candles b) 150,000 candles c) 1,500,000 candles?

2  The smallest sunspots are a) as big as Africa b) 50 times as big as Africa c) 50 million times as big as Africa?

3  We get day and night because the Sun's output is continually fluctuating: true or false?

4  The solar wind escapes through holes in the corona: true or false?

5  The corona is all you see of the Sun in a solar eclipse: true or false?

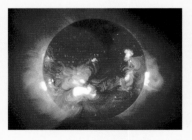

Answers
1. c) 2. b) 3. False 4. True 5. True

# The night sky

## How many stars are there in the sky?

WITHOUT A TELESCOPE, you can probably see almost two thousand stars in the sky at night if your eyesight is reasonably good. With the most powerful telescopes of all, it is possible to see many millions. But even this is just a tiny fraction of all the stars in the Universe. Astronomers guess that there are perhaps 200 billion billion altogether, most of them as big or bigger than our Sun.

▼ Observatory

*Because the world is turning, observatory telescopes have to turn too to follow the pattern of stars. So the telescope here is mounted on a turntable, and the roof turns with it. The dish to the right is a radio telescope.*

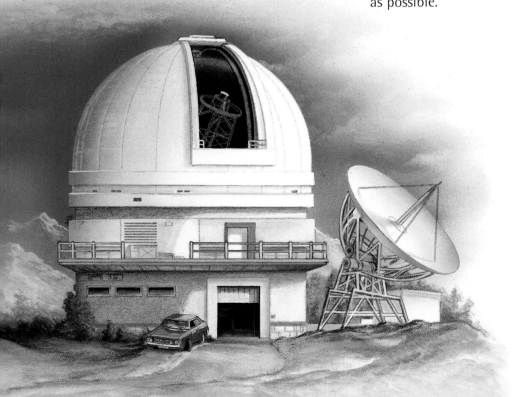

## What is an observatory?

An observatory is a place where astronomers study the night sky. Although some are located near cities for convenience, the air near cities is dirty and the light from cities makes night viewing hard. So most observatories are situated high on mountaintops, far away from cities, to give as clear a view as possible.

## What can you see in the night sky?

The biggest and brightest thing is the Moon. Everything else is just pinpoints of light to the naked eye. Most are stars. But you can also see five of the planets—Mercury, Venus, Mars, Jupiter, and Saturn—if you look at the right time. Occasionally, you may see comets and meteors shooting through the sky. The pale band across the middle of the sky called the Milky Way is actually a concentration of the stars of our own local Galaxy.

## How powerful are astronomers' telescopes?

In the last century, the most distant objects astronomers could see were about 15,000 light years away. Now powerful telescopes enable them to see galaxies 13 billion light years away. If it could focus on nearby things, a telescope this powerful would enable you to read this book from well over 300 feet (90m) away.

## How do astronomers study the night sky?

In the past, they would stare at it for hours on end through a telescope, recording where every pinpoint of light was. Nowadays, the view through the telescope is usually recorded electronically, and astronomers study the electronic image on a computer screen.

January

July

◀ **Night sky**
*The pattern of stars in the night sky is fixed, and has hardly changed since prehistoric times. But as the Earth moves, so we see a changing view of the pattern. So the pattern of stars gradually arcs through the sky during every night as the Earth turns. Each night, the pattern begins slightly further on. Only after a year, when the Earth has completed its journey, does the pattern start in the same place again.*

## What are radio telescopes?

The stars are beaming a range of radiation at us. Some, called visible light, is the light we can see. Most is invisible, with wavelengths too long or too short for our eyes. But though we can't see them, special telescopes can pick them up and so see much more of the stars than we could by visible light alone. Radio telescopes are telescopes that respond to radio waves. They use dishes to focus the rays rather than lenses, and the dishes are often 100s of yards across. Other telescopes respond to radiation bands such as microwaves and X-rays.

## What are space telescopes?

Looking at the night sky through our atmosphere is like looking through frosted glass. So astronomers send up electronic telescopes on satellites to get a clear view into space. The most famous is the Hubble Space Telescope, launched in1990.

## Can you see other planets?

Until recently the only planets known were those around our Sun, but astronomers have now observed a few very big planets circling around other stars too.

▼ **Gazing at the sky**
*A small telescope enables amateur astronomers to see much dimmer stars.*

# QUIZ

1 What is light pollution?

2 The SOHO space telescope is targeted on a) the Moon b) Uranus c) the Sun?

3 Which famous scientist was the first to look at the night sky through a telescope?

4 With a powerful telescope, you can see the equipment left behind on the Moon by the Apollo missions: true or false?

5 A light year is the distance light travels in a year: true or false?

6 Where is the largest telescope in the world being built?

Answers
1. The light from cities that makes it hard to see the night sky 2. c) 3. Galileo 4. False 5. True 6. Paranal in northern Chile

129

# Space travel

## Why do you need a rocket to go into space?

**T**O ESCAPE FROM THE PULL OF EARTH'S GRAVITY demands the power that only a rocket can provide. But traveling through the emptiness of space doesn't. So spacecraft are usually boosted into space by powerful launch vehicles–rockets designed to fall away in stages when the spacecraft is on its way.

### How do rockets work in space?

There is nothing to push on in space, but rockets move forward because the burning gas swells inside the rocket burners. As it swells, the gas pushes the rocket forward.

### ▼ Lunar module

*The lunar module was the small part of the Apollo 11 spacecraft that detached to carry astronauts Neil Armstrong and Buzz Aldrin down to the Moon's surface for the first Moon landing in 1969.*

### When was the first space flight?

The first space flight was made in October 1957 by Russia's *Sputnik 1*. The second, a month later, launched a dog called Laika into space in *Sputnik 2*. Sadly, Laika never came back.

### What is the space shuttle?

Early spacecraft were used for one flight only. The space shuttle is a reusable spacecraft. It is launched on the back of rockets like all spacecraft, but glides back to Earth and lands just like an aeroplane, and so can be used for missions again and again.

### ▶ Rocket power

*Some rockets such as boosters burn a solid rubbery fuel, but most are powered by liquid fuel. Since this only burns with oxygen, the rocket also carries a tank of liquid oxygen. The fuel and the oxygen mix in a combustion chamber, then an igniter sets them alight.*

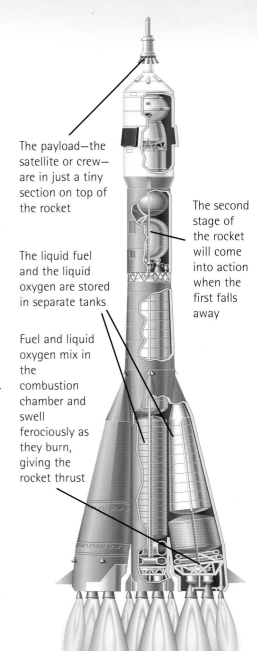

The payload—the satellite or crew—are in just a tiny section on top of the rocket

The liquid fuel and the liquid oxygen are stored in separate tanks

Fuel and liquid oxygen mix in the combustion chamber and swell ferociously as they burn, giving the rocket thrust

The second stage of the rocket will come into action when the first falls away

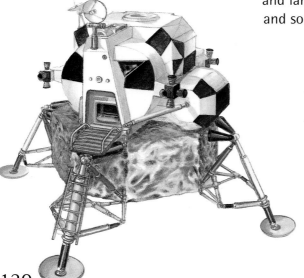

## ▶ Men on the Moon

*Astronaut Neil Armstrong waves during the Moon landing of July 21, 1969—the first manned landing on another world.*

## ▼ Space shuttle in action

*The space shuttle can be used for anything from ferrying scientists to space labs, to repairing satellites.*

## Why are things weightless in space?

Astronauts orbiting the Earth float around as if they are weightless. In fact, they are not, but the spacecraft is hurtling around the Earth so fast it counteracts the effect of gravity. It is as if the astronauts were in a lift falling so fast they float off the ground.

## Where can astronauts go?

Except for the manned missions to the Moon, all the spacecraft that have been sent off to explore the planets are robot craft, guided automatically by computer, and by radio signals from Earth. They have to be automatic, because it is very hard to bring them back to Earth. The farthest humans are likely to go is Mars.

## How many planets have spacecraft been to?

The first successful planetary spacecraft was *Mariner 2*, which flew past Venus in 1962. *Mariner 10* reached Mercury in 1974. The *Vikings 1* and *2* landed on Mars in 1976. The *Voyager* spacecraft flew past Jupiter (1979), Saturn (1980-81), Uranus (1986), and Neptune (1989) before heading out of the solar system. So only Pluto has not been visited.

## What are space stations?

Space stations are bases in space where astronauts can live and work. The Russian *Mir* has been orbiting the Earth since 1986, and the crew is replaced every two or three months. The giant ISS (International Space Station) is being built now and should be launched in 2002.

## How do satellites stay up?

By circling the Earth so fast that they never come down—like a ball thrown very hard. The closer they are to Earth, the faster they have to go.

# QUIZ

1 Who was the first man in space?

2 What did Neil Armstrong say when he stepped onto the Moon?

3 You can see TV pictures from Mars live over the Internet: true or false?

4 To escape Earth's gravity, spacecraft need to travel at least: a) 240 mph (400km/h) b) 2,400 mph (4,000km/h) c) 24,000 mph (40,000km/h)?

5 There is a Russian space station orbiting Venus: true or false?

6 How many manned missions to the Moon were there a) 1 b) 6 c) 22?

7 Who was the first man to walk in space?

Answers
1. Yuri Gagarin in 1961
2. "One small step for a man; one giant leap for mankind"
3. True 4. c) 5. False 6. b)
7. Alexei Leonov in 1965

# Satellites

## What are satellites?

**S**ATELLITES ARE OBJECTS that orbit (circle) around planets. There are natural satellites, like our Moon, and the moons that orbit planets such as Jupiter and Saturn. But in the past few decades, we have launched more and more man-made satellites. These tiny spacecraft are designed to stay in space orbiting the Earth to perform all kinds of tasks, from land use surveys to speeding up worldwide telephone communications.

▶ **Satellite**
*Most satellites get their power from panels of solar cells that turn sunlight into electricity. The panels are hinged to ensure they always face the Sun. Many satellites also have little gas jets to turn the satellite around and ensure it is positioned exactly right.*

## Are all satellite orbits the same?

No. The orbit chosen for a satellite depends on its purpose. Many satellites are launched into what is called a low orbit, about 180 miles (300km) above the Earth. A low orbit satellite circles the Earth in about 90 minutes. Low-orbit satellites cost the least to launch, since it requires a low power rocket to get them up. To get a satellite into a high orbit—above 18,000 miles (30,000km)—the satellite has to be launched first into a high orbit with one set of rockets. A second set then fires to steer it into the correct orbit.

## When were the first satellites launched?

The first artificial satellite was the *Sputnik 1* launched by the Soviet Union in 1957. Three years later, the *Tiros 1*, the first weather satellite was launched. Then in 1962, the *Telstar* satellite beamed the first live television pictures across the Atlantic.

## How do satellites stay up?

The Earth's gravity stops satellites flying off into space, but they stay up because they are moving too fast through space to fall back to Earth. To stay in orbit, the satellite must fly fast enough not to fall but not so fast that it whizzes off into space. Gravity gets weaker further from the Earth, so the higher the orbit, the slower the satellite needs to fly to stay up.

## Why do they bother with high orbits?

It costs a lot to launch a satellite into a high orbit. But an orbit 22,187 miles (35,786km) above the Earth takes exactly 24 hours. If a satellite in this orbit is above the equator, it always stays above the same place on the ground. This "geostationary" orbit is used for many weather and communications satellites.

132

◀ **Orbiting satellite**
*There are now hundreds of observation satellites in space designed to look back down on Earth, for anything from science to spying. Cameras on board spy satellites can now give such high resolution that they can pick out individual buildings and even people.*

▶ **Land and sea**
*Most satellite photos are in artificial colors to penetrate the atmosphere better.*

# QUIZ

1 **About how many satellites are launched every year: a) 10 b) 30 c) 100?**

2 **Satellite measurements have shown that there are hills and valleys on the ocean surface: true or false?**

3 **You can see some satellites in space with the naked eye: true or false?**

4 **How many satellites are there in space: a) 170 b) 550 c) more than 1,500?**

5 **The Pentagon (in Washington) knows exactly where every single satellite is all the time: true or false?**

6 **What is the launch path of a satellite called?**

7 **What kind of orbit do TV satellites have?**

### What's a polar orbit?
Polar orbiting satellites circle the Earth from Pole to Pole about 530 miles (850km) above the ground, covering a different strip of the surface each time around. So eventually, the satellite scans the entire surface in detail.

### How are satellites launched?
Satellites are launched into space either by rockets, or carried up by the space shuttle. The shuttle can only reach heights of a few hundred miles, so can only place satellites in low orbit. But some satellites have little rockets to move them up to a higher orbit.

### What is a communications satellite?
Communications satellites transmit around the world anything from TV pictures to telephone calls. Each word of a telephone call from, say, New York to Australia is bounced around the world off the satellite on a beam of microwaves.

### What's the GPS?
The GPS is the Global Positioning System. This is a network of satellites in space that allows people with a GPS device on land, on sea, or in the air to fix their position accurately to within a few feet.

**Answers**
1. c) 2. True 3. True
4. c) 5. True
6. Trajectory
7. Geostationary

133

# Inner planets

## What is the solar system?

THE SOLAR SYSTEM is the Sun and all the planets and other bits and pieces that circle around it. There are nine planets altogether–four rocky inner planets near the Sun including the Earth, and five farther out away from the Sun. The bits and pieces include comets, tiny lumps called asteroids, and meteors.

◄ **Mercury**

*Mercury hurtles around the Sun in just 88 days (compared to 365 for the Earth). But it takes 59 days to turn once on its axis. This means the Sun comes up only once a year. But once it's up it stays up for 176 days!*

## What are the inner planets?

The inner planets are, in order away from the Sun: Mercury, Venus, Earth, and Mars. All four are quite small compared with some of the outer planets such as Jupiter, and all four are made mostly of rock. Because they are made of rock, they have a hard surface on which a spacecraft could land, and are sometimes called the "terrestrial" (earthlike) planets. Space probes have landed on both Venus and Mars.

## How hot is Mercury?

Mercury is so near the Sun that daytime temperatures soar to 800°F (430°C), more than enough to melt lead. But its atmosphere is so thin that it loses all this heat at night, when temperatures plunge to –290°F (-180°C)!

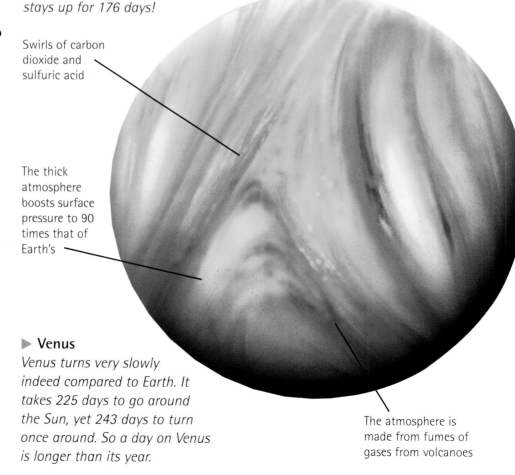

Swirls of carbon dioxide and sulfuric acid

The thick atmosphere boosts surface pressure to 90 times that of Earth's

► **Venus**

*Venus turns very slowly indeed compared to Earth. It takes 225 days to go around the Sun, yet 243 days to turn once around. So a day on Venus is longer than its year.*

The atmosphere is made from fumes of gases from volcanoes

## Why is Venus pink?

Venus is pink because it has an atmosphere so thick we can never see the surface of the planet. The atmosphere is made of white fumes of carbon dioxide and pink clouds of sulfuric acid, so it would be deadly for humans. The atmosphere is so deep that the pressure on the ground would be enough to crush a car to foil.

## Why is Venus so hot?

Venus is the hottest planet in the solar system, with surface temperatures of 890°F (470°C). The build up of carbon dioxide gas in its atmosphere has created a runaway "greenhouse effect," trapping the heat from the Sun like the panes of glass in a greenhouse.

## Why is Venus called the evening star?

Venus's thick atmosphere reflects light so well it shines like a star. But because it is quite close to the Sun, we can only see it in the evening, just after the Sun sets. By midnight, it has disappeared. But it may become visible again just before sunrise.

## What volcano is three times as high as Mt. Everest?

The surface of Mars is much more stable than Earth's and there is no rain or running water to wear down the landscape. So mountains can be very high. One volcano, called Olympus Mons, is 15 miles (24km) high—three times as high as Mt. Everest!

## Is there life on Mars?

When the Viking space probes landed on Mars in the 1970s, they found it completely lifeless. But in 1996, microscopic fossils of what might be miniviruses were found in a meteor from Mars. Future space probes may reveal microlife beneath the surface.

▼ **Mars**
*Mars is sometimes called the red planet because it is rusty. The surface has a lot of iron dust which has been oxidized (rusted) by the carbon dioxide in its atmosphere.*

Mars has small polar ice caps

Markings on Mars's surface were once thought to be signs of civilization—but they are purely geological

# QUIZ

1 Venus turns backward (the opposite way to its orbit): true or false?

2 There are ancient pyramids on Mars: true or false?

3 For a few hours during Mercury's day the Sun goes backward through the sky: true or false?

4 What is the name of the space probe that landed on Mars in 1997?

5 Which of the inner planets have moons?

6 Mercury has ice caps of yellow acid: true or false?

7 Which planet is closest to Earth?

8 Which planet has the shortest year?

9 Are there volcanoes on Venus?

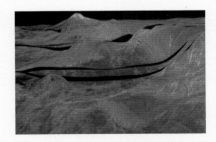

Answers
1. True 2. False 3. True 4. Mars Pathfinder 5. Mars and Earth 6. True 7. Venus 8. Mercury (88 days) 9. Yes

# Outer planets

## What are the outer planets?

THE OUTER PLANETS BEYOND MARS are, in order away from the Sun: Jupiter, Saturn, Uranus, Neptune, and Pluto. Of these, all but Pluto are very, very big—much bigger than the inner planets such as Earth and Mars. They are also made mostly of liquid gas rather than rock. So spacecraft could never land on them.

### Which is the biggest planet?

Jupiter is 88,650 miles (142,984km) across, 450,000km around and twice as heavy as all the planets put together. It is 1,300 times as big as the Earth, but only 318 times as heavy, because it is made largely of liquid hydrogen and helium.

▶ **Uranus**
*Uranus is the seventh planet out from the Sun, and rolls around it almost on its side.*

Like Saturn, Uranus has rings, but much smaller

▼ **Saturn**
*Saturn is the most beautiful of all the planets, with its shimmering pale butterscotch atmosphere and its halo of rings.*

Saturn's rings occur in broad bands, labeled with the letters A to G outward

Great Red Spot

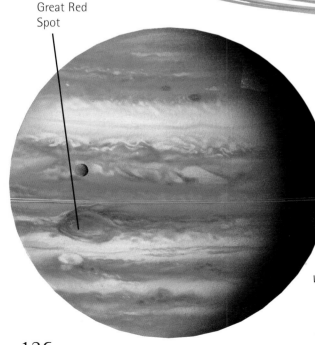

◀ **Jupiter**
*High-speed winds—six times faster than hurricanes on Earth—whir through Jupiter's atmosphere, creating bands of curling clouds on the surface—including a whirlpool called the Great Red Spot or GRS, which has been there at least 300 years.*

### What are Saturn's rings?

Saturn's rings are the planet's shining halo, first noticed in 1659 by Dutch scientist Christiaan Huygens (1629-1695). They are made of countless billions of tiny chips of ice and dust—most the size of ice cubes. The rings are incredibly thin—no more than 150 feet (45m) deep—yet they stretch more than 46,000 miles (74,200km) out into space.

## ▼ Neptune

*Neptune is the eighth planet out from the Sun—up to 2.5 billion miles (4 billion km). It is so far away from the Sun that it takes 164.79 years to go around—its year is 164.79 Earth years.*

# QUIZ

1 Which planet is farthest from the Sun?

2 Comets are made mostly of ice: true or false?

3 Saturn would float if you could find a bath big enough: true or false?

4 Which planet is named after the Roman god of the underworld?

5 The surface of Jupiter spins at 28,000 mph (45,000 km/h): true or false?

6 Saturn's moon Enceladus is made mainly of sugar: true or false?

7 On Uranus in spring, the Sun rises and sets backward: true or false?

8 Which planet has the most moons?

9 Jupiter glows like a big light bulb: true or false?

Neptune receives so little solar heat that the surface is -346°F (-210°C)

Winds of hydrogen and helium roar round at over 2,000kmh

## ▶ Pluto and Charon

*Pluto is five times smaller than Earth, and its moon Charon is almost half its size. It is so far away that it was only spotted for the first time in 1930.*

## How many moons have the outer planets?

All the outer planets except Pluto have lots of moons. Jupiter has 16, Saturn at least 19, Uranus 17, and Neptune 8. Some of them are almost as big as the planet Mercury. Saturn's moon Titan is exciting astronomers because it has an atmosphere—the only moon in the solar system with one—so may have some form of life.

## When were Uranus and Neptune discovered?

Unlike the planets farther in, Uranus and Neptune were completely unknown to ancient astronomers. They are so far away from us and so faint that they can only be seen through powerful telescopes. Uranus was discovered only in 1781, and Neptune in 1846. They were both visited by the *Voyager* space probe between 1986 and 1989.

## Why is Neptune turquoise?

Neptune and Uranus are both bluey turquoise in color because their surfaces are completely covered in deep oceans of liquid methane (the same gas you burn in ovens).

## How cold is it on Pluto?

Pluto is so far from the Sun, the Sun looks just like a star in the sky, and temperatures plunge to -364°F (-220°C). Each day on Pluto lasts 6.39 Earth days—but a year lasts 248.54 Earth years, during which time Pluto travels more than 9 billion miles (15 billion km).

**Answers**
1. Pluto 2. True 3. True
4. Pluto 5. True
6. False 7. True
8. Saturn 9. True

# Stars

## What are stars?

STARS ARE HUGE FIERY BALLS OF GAS. They shine because they are burning. Deep inside, hydrogen atoms fuse together to form helium as they are squeezed by the star's gravity. This nuclear reaction unleashes so much energy that the core of the star reaches millions of degrees and makes the surface glow–sending out light, heat, radio waves, and many other kinds of radiation.

### How big are stars?

Our Sun is an average sized star. There are "red giant" stars 20 to 100 times as big. Supergiants such as Betelgeuse are 500 times as big and 420 million miles (700 million km) across. There are also smaller stars too, such as white dwarfs smaller than the Earth and neutron stars just 9 miles (15km) across. These remnants of old stars have collapsed under their own gravity.

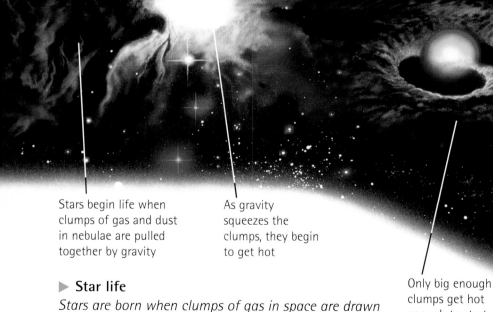

Stars begin life when clumps of gas and dust in nebulae are pulled together by gravity

As gravity squeezes the clumps, they begin to get hot

Only big enough clumps get hot enough to start the fusion reaction

Nuclear fusion begins as hydrogen atoms fuse together to make helium. The heat makes the star glow

### ▶ Star life

*Stars are born when clumps of gas in space are drawn together by their own gravity, and the middle of the clump is squeezed so hard that temperatures reach 18 million°F (10 million°C)—enough to start the nuclear fusion reaction that makes stars glow. All this happens inside vast clouds of dust and gas called nebulae.*

## What is a constellation?

Constellations are patterns made by stars that astronomers use to find their way around the night sky. There is no link at all between the stars in a constellation; it simply looks that way. They were given names like the Great Bear and Orion by astronomers long ago. There are now 88 recognized.

## Why do stars twinkle?

They twinkle because the Earth's atmosphere is never still, and starlight twinkles as the air wavers. Light from the nearby planets is not distorted as much, so they don't twinkle.

## How hot are stars?

The surface temperature of stars ranges from 6,300°F (3,500°C) to more than 72,000° (40,000°C).

## What is the brightest star?

The nearer a star is, the brighter it appears. So some of the biggest brightest stars in the Universe appear quite dim simply because they are far away. The star that seems the brightest from Earth is Sirius the Dog Star, which is 26 times brighter than the Sun. But the hypergiant Cygnus OB2 No. 12 is 810,000 times brighter than our Sun but is almost 6 billion light years away, so seems quite dim.

## What is the nearest star?

Apart from our Sun, the nearest star is the faint Proxima Centauri just over 4 light years away. The nearest visible to the naked eye is Alpha Centauri, 4.35 light years away.

If the heat made in the core pushes out as hard as gravity pulls in, the star stabilizes and burns steadily for billions of years

# QUIZ

1   What constellation is named after a fish?

2   What star shines at the dead center of the northern sky?

3   The constellation Pleiades is named after a) three sisters b) seven sisters c) twelve sisters?

4   The group of stars called the Big Dipper in the USA is called in Europe a) the Plow b) the Panhandle c) the Scythe?

5   The constellation Cygnus is named after a god who became a swan to seduce a girl: true or false?

6   The Dog Star has a companion star called the Pup Star: true or false?

7   Betelgeuse gets its name because it is the color of beetle blood: true or false?

**Answers**
1. Pisces 2. Polaris, the Pole star 3. b) 4. a) 5. True 6. True 7. False

# The life of a star

## How long do stars live?

THE BIGGEST, BRIGHTEST STARS are the shortest-lived, many surviving less than ten million years. Medium-sized stars like our Sun last much longer–ten billion years or more. Small stars may last much, much longer.

▼ **The end of a star**
*Toward the end of a star's life, its hydrogen is burned up and it shrinks to burn helium. When the helium runs out, the outer layers cool and it swells to become a red giant. The biggest stars go on swelling to become supergiants with cores so pressurized that carbon and silicon fuse to make iron.*

### Why do stars die?
Stars die when they have exhausted their vast supplies of nuclear fuel. When the hydrogen runs out, they switch to helium. When helium runs out, they quickly exhaust any remaining nuclear fuel then either blow up, shrink or go cold.

### What is a supernova?
A supernova is a gigantic explosion that finishes off a supergiant star. For just a brief moment, the supernova flashes out with the brilliance of billions of suns. They are rare and short-lived, but there is always one somewhere in the Universe.

### What are the oldest stars?
The oldest stars are not stars at all but look like them because they are so far away. Some of these "quasi-stellar radio objects" or quasars, are so far away, the light we see left them 13 billion years ago.

Once iron forms in its core, the star does not release energy but absorbs it

## What are nebulae?

Nebulae are giant clouds of gas and dust spread throughout the galaxies. Some of them can be seen through telescopes because they shine faintly as they reflect starlight. Others, called dark nebulae, can only be seen because they hide the stars behind with an inky black patch. It is in these dark nebulae that stars are born.

The collapse of a supergiant star triggers an explosion like a gigantic nuclear bomb called a supernova

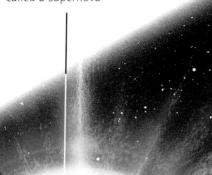

As it absorbs energy, the star suddenly and catastrophically collapses in a few seconds to little bigger than a planet

## What is a white dwarf?

White dwarfs are the small white stars formed as stars smaller than our Sun lose their surface gas altogether and shrink. Yet they are much bigger than neutron stars, which are all that is left of a supergiant star after a supernova explosion. Neutron stars are unimaginably dense.

# QUIZ

1 Supernova can send out more energy in a few seconds than our Sun in 200 million years: true or false?

2 Stars called pulsars which beam out regular radio signals are called LGMs. LGM stands for: a) Little Green Man b) Low Gas Matter c) Light Generating Masses?

3 A teaspoonful of neutron star weighs a) 10 tons b) ten million tons c) ten billion tons?

4 Red dwarf stars glow red because they are made of coal: true or false?

5 Astronomers have discovered alcohol in the clouds called nebulae: true or false?

**Answers**
1. True 2. a), because the signals are so regular, it was once thought they might be aliens 3. c) 4. False 5. True

# Galaxies

## What are galaxies?

OUR SUN IS JUST ONE of a vast concentration of more than 100 billion stars, arranged in a shape like a fried egg, more than 100,000 light-years across. This huge star city is called the Milky Way or the Galaxy because we see it as a pale band across the night sky–the word "galaxy" comes from the Greek for milky. But earlier this century, astronomers realized that the Galaxy is not the only star city in the universe. In fact, there are billions of similar star groups scattered throughout space. These are also called galaxies (with a small "g").

### Why is the Milky Way just a band across the sky?

Because we are seeing it edge on. We are out on one edge, looking in toward the center and the Milky Way in the sky is the narrow layer of stars stretching away from us. If we could travel millions of light years out at right angles to the Milky Way, we would see that it is indeed spiral.

### Where is the Earth?

The Earth and the solar system are on one of the Galaxy's spiral arms, about 30,000 light years out from the center.

▼ **The Milky Way**

*The Milky Way is the pale, blotchy white band that stretches right across the night sky. A powerful telescope reveals that is made of countless stars. It is actually an edge on view of our Galaxy.*

The trailing arms of stars are embedded in a ball of dark matter

The Galaxy is sweeping the Sun and other stars around at 60 million mph (100 million km/h)

There is a concentration of stars at the heart of the Galaxy

142

Barred spiral
galaxy

Irregular
galaxy

Spiral
galaxy

Elliptical
galaxy

## ▶ Galactic shapes
*There are four main kinds of galaxy, but the distinction between them is not always completely clear.*

## Is the Galaxy turning?
Yes, it is whirling round so fast it sweeps us along at 60 million mph (100 million km/h)! We go once round the Galaxy, a journey of almost 100,000 light years in just 200 million years. But we are so much a part of the Galaxy we only know we are moving by watching distant galaxies.

The Sun is just one of the stars in the Galaxy, located on an arm 30,000 light-years out

## What is a spiral galaxy?
A spiral galaxy is one of the four kinds of galaxy. It has spiraling arms of stars like a giant Catherine wheel. They trail because the galaxy is rotating rapidly. Our Galaxy is a spiral galaxy.

## Where is the next galaxy?
The Galaxy's nearest neighbor is the only other galaxy you can see with the naked eye, the Andromeda galaxy, which is about 2.9 million light years away. But there are 30 or so galaxies in our own neighborhood, called the Local Group, which is itself part of a cluster of 3,000 galaxies.

## Is there anything else but stars in a galaxy?
The Milky Way and other spiral galaxies look flat like a fried egg. In fact, they may be shaped more like burgers—and all we are seeing is the meat in the burger. The bread is mysterious stuff called Dark Matter, because it can't be seen or detected in any way. We only know it is there because of the way it's gravity affects the stars. It may be that more than 90 percent of the mass of the Universe is dark matter.

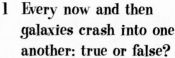
# QUIZ

1  Every now and then galaxies crash into one another: true or false?

2  The Large Magellanic Cloud is a) a nebula b) a kind of thundercloud c) a galaxy?

3 What creatures dominated the Earth the last time our spiral arm of the Galaxy was in the same place ?

4  The biggest structure in the Universe is the Great Wall of galaxies. It is a) 4,000 b) 4 million c) 500 million light-years thick?

5  Which astronomer first showed there were galaxies beyond our own a) Copernicus b) Herschel c) Hubble?

**Answers**
1. True  2. c)  3. Dinosaurs  4. c)  5. c) Edwin Hubble (1889-1953), along with other astronomers in the 1920s

# Distant objects

### Candle power
*The farther away a candle is, the more dim it looks. The same is true of stars—and this is how astronomers measure how far away the stars are.*

## How big is the Universe?

BIGGER THAN YOU CAN possibly imagine. Venus, the nearest planet, is 25 million miles (40 million km) away at its nearest. The planet Pluto is 3.7 billion miles (6 billion km) away. The nearest galaxy beyond our own is 19 quadrillion miles (30,000 trillion km) away. The farthest object astronomers can see is 400,000 times farther away still—and the Universe must stretch way beyond that, and is getting bigger by the second.

### How are distances given in space?
Distances are so great in space that they can't be measured in miles or kilometers. Instead, they are measured in light-years and parsecs. A parsec is 3.26 light-years.

A black hole is a place where gravity is so strong it sucks everything in, even light

### What's a light year?
Light is the fastest thing in the Universe, travelling at almost 186,000 miles (300,000km) a second. It gets to the Moon in the blink of an eye. It takes eight minutes for light to reach us from the Sun and four YEARS to reach us from the nearest star. A light-year is the distance light travels in a year, which is about 600 billion miles (one trillion km)!

Black holes form when a star or galaxy gets so dense that it collapses under the pull of its own gravity

### Quasar
*Quasars are so bright we can see them billions of light years away. Their energy may come from gas being sucked into a black hole in their midst.*

144

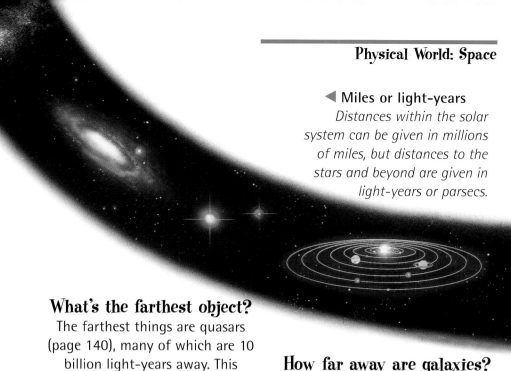

◀ **Miles or light-years**
*Distances within the solar system can be given in millions of miles, but distances to the stars and beyond are given in light-years or parsecs.*

## What's the farthest object?

The farthest things are quasars (page 140), many of which are 10 billion light-years away. This means we are seeing them as they were 10 billion years ago—more than five billion years before the Earth was formed, and shortly after the dawn of the Universe.

## How do they measure how far a star is?

Distances to nearby stars can be measured by the parallax method. As the Earth circles the Sun, a nearby star seems to shift a little compared to stars farther away, as our viewpoint changes slightly. By measuring how much it shifts, we can work out how far off it is.

## How do they measure how far to more distant stars?

The further away a star is, the dimmer it looks. But some stars burn brightly while others glimmer. So it's hard to tell if a dim star is far away or just feeble. But the color of a star shows how bright it really is. If you know how bright a star really is from its color, you can work out how far away it is by comparing this with how bright it looks.

## How far away are galaxies?

Beyond about 30,000 light-years, stars are too indistinct to work out the color accurately. So for objects at this distance, we look for "standard candles"—that is, a star whose brightness we know. The dimmer it looks compared to how bright it should look, the farther away it must be. Standard candles include supernova and fluctuating stars called cepheid variables.

## What is red shift?

When a galaxy is moving rapidly away from us, the waves of light from it become stretched out—that is, they become redder. The greater this red shift, the faster the galaxy must be moving away from us.

## Are the galaxies moving?

Studying red shifts has shown that every galaxy is moving away from us. The farther away it is, the faster it is receding. The most distant galaxies are receding at almost the speed of light.

# QUIZ

1  At its nearest, the Moon is 100,000 miles (160,000km) away: true or false?

2  The distance to the Moon is measured with laser beams bounced off mirrors left on the surface by space probes: true or false?

3  The sun is about 93 million miles (150 million km) away: true or false?

4  How many light-years away is Andromeda?

5  The star Deneb is 3,200 light-years away. Who was ruling in Egypt at the same time as we see it?

6  How soon could you get to the Sun and back at the speed of light?

# The Big Bang

## How did the Universe begin?

THE UNIVERSE began with the biggest explosion of all time, called the Big Bang. One moment there was just an unimaginably small, incredibly hot little ball. A moment later, the Universe burst into existence with a gigantic explosion. Within a split second, all the forces that shape the Universe were created and so too was all the matter. The explosion was so big that material is still hurtling away from it in all directions at astonishing speeds.

### What was the early Universe like?

The early Universe was very small, but it contained all the matter and energy in the Universe today. It was a dense and chaotic soup of tiny particles and forces—and instead of the four forces scientists know today, there was just one superforce. But this original Universe lasted only a moment. After just three trillionths of a trillionth of a trillionth of a second, the superforce split to create the separate forces we know today.

# Can you see the Big Bang?

Astronomers can see the galaxies hurtling away from us in all directions. They can also see the afterglow of the Big Bang—as low level microwave radiation coming toward us from all over space. This is called microwave background radiation. In 1992, the Cosmic Background Explorer (COBE) made a complete map of the background.

# When did the galaxies and stars form?

Galaxies and stars probably began to form about 300 million years after the Big Bang, from curdled lumps of hydrogen and helium gas. Some astronomers think they formed as large clumps and broke into smaller clumps. Others think they formed as clumps packed tighter and tighter.

# What will happen in the future?

No one knows if the Universe will go on growing. It all depends on how much matter it contains. If there is more than the "critical density," gravity will put a brake in its expansion, and it may soon begin to contract again to end in a Big Crunch. If there is about the same, it may already be in a "steady state" neither expanding nor contracting. If there is much less than the critical density, it will go on expanding forever. This is called the Open Universe.

# How old is the Universe?

We know that the Universe is getting bigger at a certain rate by observing how fast distant galaxies are moving. By working out how long it took everything to expand to where it is now, we can wind back the clock to the time when the Universe was very small. This suggests the Universe began somewhere between 13 and 15 billion years ago. However, studies of globular clusters of stars suggest some stars in our galaxy may be 18 billion years old.

# What was there before the Universe began?

No one has the remotest idea. Some people think there was a weird ocean, beyond space and time, full of potential universes continually bursting into life. Ours was one of the successful ones. There may be others.

# How do scientists know what the early Universe was like?

They don't for certain, but they can get a good idea from mathematical calculations based on laws of physics today, and from experiments with huge machines called colliders and particle accelerators. These recreate conditions in the early Universe by using magnets to accelerate particles to astonishing speeds in a special tunnel, then smashing them all together.

# QUIZ

1 What was the first chemical element to form?

2 Which scientist wrote a book called "A Brief History of Time"?

3 How old is the Earth?

4 The Universe is getting bigger, but only the space between the galaxies is stretching: true or false?

5 Which formed first: the Milky Way or the Sun?

6 Two of the four basic forces in the Universe hold the nuclei of atoms together. What are the other two?

7 Is the Andromeda galaxy getting nearer to us or farther away?

8 Astronomers can detect sounds from the far side of the Universe: true or false?

**Answers**
1. Hydrogen 2. Stephen Hawking 3. 4.6 billion years 4. True 5. The Milky Way 6. Gravity and electromagnetism 7. Farther, like all galaxies 8. False, there are no sounds in space

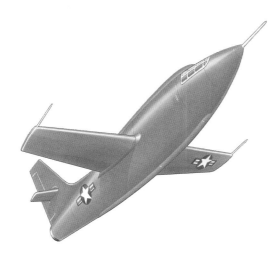

What substance has the highest melting point?

What did Newton learn from an apple?

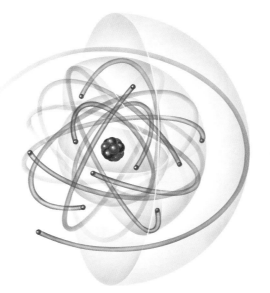

How big are atoms?

Why are racing bicycles made of light materials?

Why don't lakes freeze solid?

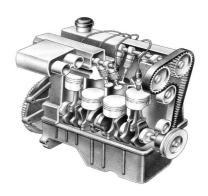

What frog makes Indian arrows deadly?

148

Why is laser light special?

# Science

Can sound travel in a vacuum?

Why does hair go frizzy?

What is virtual reality?

# Matter

## What is matter?

**M**ATTER IS EVERY SUBSTANCE in the universe—everything that is not simply empty space. There are three different forms or "states" of matter—solid like a brick, liquid like water, and gas like air. Every substance can change from one state to another and back again, providing the temperature and pressure are right.

▲ **Freezing**
*When a liquid cools, the molecules slow down enough for regular bonds to grow between them. When water freezes to snowflakes, beautiful crystals form.*

▼ **Water cycle**
*Water is the only substance to exist naturally on Earth in all three states—solid ice, liquid water, and the gas water vapor. Water is called water vapor when it is a gas; steam is actually lots of tiny drops of water.*

### What is a solid?

When a substance is solid, it has strength and a definite shape. Every substance is made from minute bits called molecules, much, much too small to see. In a solid, the molecules are bonded together firmly in a regular structure. Like all molecules, they are moving all the time, but in a solid molecules simply vibrate on the spot. The hotter it gets, the more they vibrate.

### What is a liquid?

A liquid is substance in a state like water, which flows and takes the shape of any container it is poured into. It does this because although bonds hold its molecules together, the bonds are loose enough for molecules to roll over each other like dry sand.

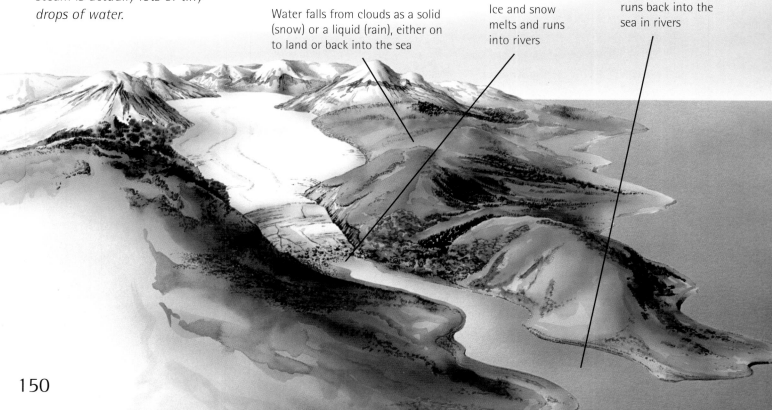

Water falls from clouds as a solid (snow) or a liquid (rain), either on to land or back into the sea

Ice and snow melts and runs into rivers

Rainwater and snow runs back into the sea in rivers

## Solid

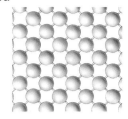

Liquid          Gas

▲ Loosening bonds

*It is the bonds between the molecules it is made from that make a substance solid, liquid, or gas. As the temperature rises, the molecules move more and the bonds get looser.*

## What is a gas?

A gas is when a substance is in a state like air. It does not have any strength, shape, or volume. The molecules move so fast that they break any bonds that might hold them together.

## What happens when things melt or boil?

When a solid melts, it turns to liquid because heat makes the molecules vibrate so much that they break the bonds that hold them together. If it gets even hotter, the molecules zoom all over the place, and some move so fast they break away from the surface of the liquid altogether, turning to gas.

As seawater is warmed by the sun, some of it evaporates (turns to vapor) and begins to rise up through the air on warm air currents

As it rises through the air and cools, water vapor condenses (turns to liquid), and forms clouds

# QUIZ

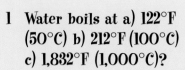

1　Water boils at a) 122°F (50°C) b) 212°F (100°C) c) 1,832°F (1,000°C)?

2　Helium has the lowest freezing point of any substance. Is it a) -458°F (-272.2°C) b) -9.5°F (12.5°C) c) 30°F (-1.1°C)?

3　Iron has the highest melting point of any metal: true or false?

4　What substance has the highest melting point?

5　What is condensation?

6　What is melting point?

7　Which metal is liquid at normal temperatures?

8　Clouds contain water in which states of matter?

# Atoms

## What is an atom?

ATOMS ARE THE TINY BITS OR "PARTICLES" of which every substance is made. They are far too small to see. Two billion of them would fit on the dot on the top of this "i." Scientists once thought they were the smallest things in the universe—and that they were tiny hard balls that could never be split or destroyed. Now they know atoms are more like clouds of energy, and are mostly empty space, dotted with even tinier "subatomic" particles.

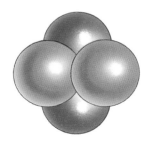

▲ Helium nucleus

*The nucleus of an atom of helium is one of the smallest—though not as small as hydrogen. It combines two protons with two neutrons.*

### What's inside an atom?

Right in the center of every atom, like a pea in a basketball, is a dense core or "nucleus" containing two kinds of tiny particle—protons and neutrons. Around the nucleus are even tinier particles called electrons, whizzing round at the speed of light.

### How big are atoms?

They are about a ten millionth of a millimeter across and weigh 100 trillionths of a trillionth of a gram. The smallest atoms of all are hydrogen atoms.

Electrons behave as if they were stacked around the nucleus in different levels, like layers of an onion. The levels are called shells

The particles of the nucleus are held together by a force called the strong nuclear force

Electrons are held to the nucleus by electrical charge—because they have an opposite electrical charge to the protons in the nucleus

The nucleus is made from particles called protons and neutrons, which are made, in turn, of even smaller particles called quarks

There is only room for a certain number of electrons in each shell

▶ Inside an atom

*Atoms don't really look this, but it is a good way to think of them. Most of an atom is empty space, but right in the center is a nucleus of protons and neutrons, held together by special nuclear forces. Around the outside whizz electrons, held in place by the opposite electrical charge on the protons.*

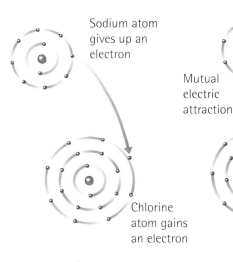

Sodium atom gives up an electron

Mutual electric attraction

Chlorine atom gains an electron

◀ **Ionic bond**

*Atoms are only stable if they have a full set of electrons in their outer shells. They can get this by bonding with other atoms to make molecules. In "ionic" bonds one atom donates an electron to the other and becomes negatively charged. The atoms are then bonded by mutual electrical attraction. This is how sodium atoms bond with chlorine atoms to make salt molecules.*

### What is an electrical charge?

Protons have a "positive" electrical charge, which just means they attract electrons. Electrons have a "negative" electrical charge, which means they attract protons. Neutrons have no charge. Most atoms have the same number of protons and electrons, so their charges balance out. The charge on electrons drives them apart. If they were not attracted to the protons, the electrons on an atom would fly off.

### What is an ion?

An ion is an atom that has either lost one or more electrons, making it positively charged (cation) or gained a few, making it negatively charged (anion).

▶ **Covalent bond**

*Atoms are only stable when they have a full set of electrons in their outer shell. Atoms which have too many or too few can get a full set by sharing electrons with other atoms. This makes a "covalent" bond.*

### What are molecules?

Some atoms cannot exist by themselves, and so join up with others—either of the same kind, or with others to form chemical compounds. A molecule is the smallest particle of a substance that can exist on its own.

### How many kinds of sub-atomic particle are there?

At least 200, besides electrons, protons and neutrons. But most are created in special conditions and last only a split second.

### What are the smallest particles?

Protons are made of tiny particles called quarks. Electrons are also tiny. But the smallest of all are neutrinos.

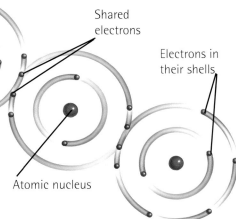

Shared electrons

Electrons in their shells

Atomic nucleus

# QUIZ

1 The smallest atom is hydrogen, which has one proton in its nucleus. Meitnerium is the biggest. It has a) 30 protons b) 40 protons c) more than 100 protons?

2 Who first split an atomic nucleus in 1919 a) Newton b) Dalton c) Rutherford?

3 Scientists think quarks are stuck together by gluons: true or false?

4 All particles are either quarks or leptons: true or false?

5 An atom with a full outer shell of electrons, like argon, does not react with others: true or false?

6 A new chemical element is made when an atom gains a proton: true or false?

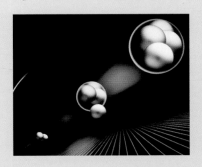

Answers
1. c) 2. c) 3. True 4. True
5. True 6. True

# Chemicals

## What are chemical elements?

CHEMICAL ELEMENTS ARE substances that cannot be split up into other substances. Gold is an element because it cannot be split. Water is not, because it can be split into the elements hydrogen and oxygen. What makes each element different are the atoms it is made from. Each element is made from atoms with a certain number of protons in their nucleus. Atoms of gold have 79 protons in their nucleus; atoms of hydrogen have 1.

### How many elements?

85 or so occur naturally. But scientists have found a further 25 or so, bringing the total so far identified to 112.

### What is the periodic table?

Devised by the chemist John Dalton (1766-1844) the Periodic Table is a chart on which all the elements can be arranged according to the number of protons in the nucleus. Columns are called Groups, rows are called Periods. Each Period contains elements with atoms which have the same number of electron shells. In each Period, the number of protons (and so the number of electrons) in the atom goes up one by one. Elements in the same Group have the same number of electrons in the outer shell of their atoms, and so have similar properties.

▶ The Periodic Table

*The Periodic Table arranges all the elements in Periods (rows) and Groups (columns). The colors show some of the major kinds of element, including metals and transition elements.*

## What are the noble gases?

Noble gases are the elements in Group 0, on the far right of the Table. Their outer electron shells have a full complement of electrons. This means they rarely react with other substances. This is why they are sometimes also called inert gases. The noble gases argon and xenon are often used in light bulbs, because the light bulb's filament will get hot in them without burning.

Hydrogen has the lightest and simplest atoms, with just one proton, one neutron and one electron

Metals are "electropositive" elements, which means they lose negatively charged electrons easily—which is why they conduct electricity well

Group 1 are metal elements with just one electron in their outer shells — so are very reactive

The actinides are 15 radioactive elements like radium and plutonium that get their name from actinium

| | | | | | | |
|---|---|---|---|---|---|---|
| H<br>hydrogen<br>1 | | | | | | |
| Li<br>lithium<br>3 | Be<br>beryllium<br>4 | | | | | |
| Na<br>sodium<br>11 | Mg<br>magnesium<br>12 | | | | | |
| K<br>potassium<br>19 | Ca<br>calcium<br>20 | Sc<br>scandium<br>21 | Ti<br>titanium<br>22 | V<br>vanadium<br>23 | Cr<br>chromium<br>24 | Mn<br>manganese<br>25 |
| Rb<br>rubidium<br>37 | Sr<br>strontium<br>38 | Y<br>yttrium<br>39 | Zr<br>zirconium<br>40 | Nb<br>niobium<br>41 | Mo<br>molybdenum<br>42 | Tc<br>technetium<br>43 |
| Cs<br>caesium<br>55 | Ba<br>barium<br>56 | Lu<br>lutetium<br>71 | Hf<br>hafnium<br>72 | Ta<br>tantalum<br>73 | W<br>tungsten<br>74 | Re<br>rhenium<br>75 |
| Fr<br>francium<br>87 | Ra<br>radium<br>88 | Lr<br>lawrencium<br>103 | Rf<br>rutherfordium<br>104 | Db<br>dubnium<br>105 | Sg<br>seaborgium<br>106 | Bh<br>bohrium<br>107 |
| La<br>lanthanum<br>57 | Ce<br>cerium<br>58 | Pr<br>praseodymium<br>59 | Nd<br>neodymium<br>60 | Pm<br>promethium<br>61 | | |
| Ac<br>actinium<br>89 | Th<br>thorium<br>90 | Pa<br>protactinium<br>91 | U<br>uranium<br>92 | Np<br>neptunium<br>93 | | |

## Why are some elements reactive?

Elements are reactive if they readily gain or lose electrons. The farther to the left in the Table they are, the more reactive they are. Group 1 metals such as sodium and potassium are very reactive.

## What is a metal?

Metals are hard, dense, and shiny substances that ring when you hit them with another metal. They also conduct heat and electricity well.

## What is a compound?

Compounds are substances made from two or more elements joined together. Every molecule (smallest particle) in a compound is made from the same combination of atoms. Molecules of sodium chloride, for instance, are one sodium atom joined to one chlorine. Compounds have different properties to the elements that make them up. Sodium spits when put in water; chlorine is a thick green gas. Yet sodium chloride is table salt.

Group 5 is nonmetals such as nitrogen at the top, but gets more and more metallic lower down with antimony and bismuth

Group 7 is the halogens— nonmetals such as chlorine and iodine

Group 4 includes silicon and carbon, which form more compounds than any other elements

Group 0 is the noble gases such as neon, which have full outer electron shells and are unreactive

| | | | | | He helium 2 |
|---|---|---|---|---|---|
| B boron 5 | C carbon 6 | N nitrogen 7 | O oxygen 8 | F fluorine 9 | Ne neon 10 |
| Al aluminium 13 | Si silicon 14 | P phosphorus 15 | S sulfur 16 | Cl chlorine 17 | Ar argon 18 |

| Fe iron 26 | Co cobalt 27 | Ni nickel 28 | Cu copper 29 | Zn zinc 30 | Ga gallium 31 | Ge germanium 32 | As arsenic 33 | Se selenium 34 | Br bromine 35 | Kr krypton 36 |
|---|---|---|---|---|---|---|---|---|---|---|
| Ru ruthenium 44 | Rh rhodium 45 | Pd palladium 46 | Ag silver 47 | Cd cadmium 48 | In indium 49 | Sn tin 50 | Sb antimony 51 | Te tellurium 52 | I iodine 53 | Xe xenon 54 |
| Os osmium 76 | Ir iridium 77 | Pt platinum 78 | Au gold 79 | Hg mercury 80 | Ti thalium 81 | Pb lead 82 | Bi bismuth 83 | Po polonium 84 | At astatine 85 | Rn radon 86 |
| Hs hassium 108 | Mt meitnerium 109 | Uun unununilium 110 | Uuu unununium 111 | Uub ununbium 112 | ? | ?? | | | | |

| Sm samarium 62 | Eu europium 63 | Gd gadolinium 64 | Tb terbium 65 | Dy dysprosium 66 | Ho holmium 67 | Er erbium 68 | Tm thulium 69 | Yb ytterbium 70 |
|---|---|---|---|---|---|---|---|---|
| Pu plutonium 94 | Am americium 95 | Cm curium 96 | Bk berkelium 97 | Cf californium 98 | Es einsteinium 99 | Fm fermium 100 | Md mendelevium 101 | No nobelium 102 |

# QUIZ

1 Which two elements is water made from?

2 Is table salt an element?

3 Who discovered the element radium?

4 Diamonds, coal, lead pencils, and racing cars are made from the same element. Which is it?

5 What is the main element in the air besides oxygen?

6 What is the second lightest element?

7 Which has the most protons in its atoms: gold or lead?

8 Krypton is a highly reactive gas: true or false?

9 Chemists can try out new molecules on computer screens: true or false?

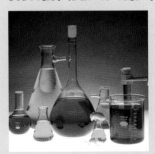

Answers
1. Hydrogen & oxygen 2. No, a compound 3. Marie Curie 4. Carbon 5. Nitrogen 6. Helium 7. Lead 8. False 9. True

# Heat and energy

## What is heat?

**H**EAT IS A FORM OF ENERGY–the energy of molecules moving. The faster they move, the hotter it is. When you put your hand over a heater, the warmth you feel is actually an assault by billions of fast-moving air molecules, spurred along by even faster moving molecules in the heater. We measure how hot something is by its temperature. But temperature is not the same as heat. Heat is the combined energy of all the moving molecules. Temperature is simply a measure of how fast the molecules are moving.

◀ **Thermometer**
*In a thermometer like this, the temperature is shown by how far the liquid in the bulb at the bottom expands and rises up the tube.*

▼ **Fire**
*Fire is a chemical reaction in which one substance gets so hot that it combines with oxygen in the air. The reaction releases so much energy that the atoms send out rays of light, making bright, dancing flames.*

## How does heat move?

Heat moves in three ways: conduction, convection and radiation. Conduction involves heat spreading from hot areas to cold areas by direct contact, as moving particles knock into one another. Convection is when warm air or water rises as it expands and gets lighter. Radiation is heat rays—invisible rays of infrared light.

## How is temperature measured?

Temperature is measured with a thermometer. Some thermometers have a metal strip that bends according to how hot it is. Most hold a liquid, such as mercury, in a tube. As the air warms, the liquid expands, and its level rises in the tube. The level of the liquid indicates the temperature.

## What are Centigrade and Fahrenheit?

These are two scales for measuring temperature. Centigrade is also called Celsius. Water freezes at 32°F (Fahrenheit) and 0°C (Centigrade). It boils at 212°F and 100°C. To convert from °F to °C, first subtract 32 and divide by nine then multiply by five. To change °C to °F, divide by five and multiply by nine, then add 32.

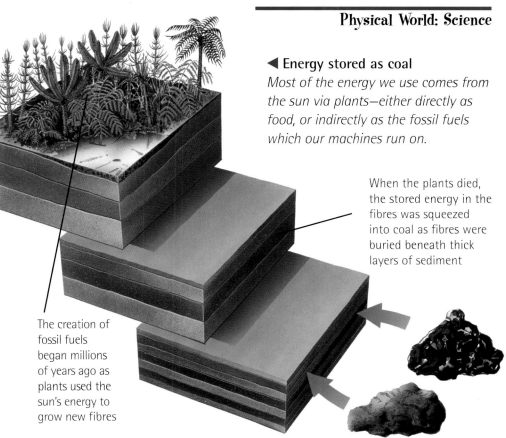

### ◀ Energy stored as coal
*Most of the energy we use comes from the sun via plants—either directly as food, or indirectly as the fossil fuels which our machines run on.*

When the plants died, the stored energy in the fibres was squeezed into coal as fibres were buried beneath thick layers of sediment

The creation of fossil fuels began millions of years ago as plants used the sun's energy to grow new fibres

## What is energy?
Energy is the capacity to make things happen or, as scientists put it, "work." It takes many forms. Heat energy boils water. Chemical energy fuels cars and airplanes. Electrical energy drives all kinds of small machines and keeps lights glowing. Most of our energy comes from the sun, mostly indirectly either from plants or as fossil fuels (see page 21).

## What happens to energy?
Energy can neither be created nor destroyed. When you use energy, you simply convert it from one form to another. When you run, you simply change the chemical energy of your muscles into heat energy, which is lost from the body. When energy is converted, there is always the same amount of energy after as before.

●

## What's absolute zero?
Absolute zero is the coldest possible temperature—at which atoms and molecules stop moving altogether. This is -459°F or -273.15°C, or 0 on the Kelvin scale.

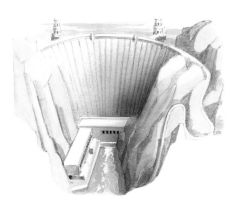

### ◀ Movement to electricity
*Hydroelectric power stations convert the energy of moving water into electrical energy.*

# QUIZ

1  The highest temperature ever measured, in a nuclear fusion experiment, is
a) 54,000°F (30,000°C)
b) 900,000°F (500,000°C)
c) 72 million°F (40 million°C)?

2  The highest air temperature recorded, in Libya, is 199°F (92°C): true or false?

3  The lowest air temperature ever recorded, -127°F (-88°C), was in Alaska: true or false?

4  What do solar cells do?

5  Energy is a form of mass: true or false?

6  On the Kelvin scale used by scientists water freezes at 273.15 K: true or false?

7  How much of the world's energy comes from coal a) 12% b) 27% c) 45%?

# Forces

## What is a force?

**A** FORCE IS JUST A PUSH OR A PULL. Some forces are invisible, like gravity, which holds us to the ground. Some are visible, like a kick. But they all work by making something go faster, slow down or change shape.

▲ **Isaac Newton**
*Isaac Newton (1643-1727) was the great scientist who developed the idea of gravity and other forces.*

### What did Newton learn from an apple?

According to the great 17th-century scientist Sir Isaac Newton, his ideas about the force of gravity came to him as he was sitting under an apple tree. When he saw an apple fall, it occurred to him that the apple was not simply falling, but being pulled to the ground by an invisible force, which he called gravity.

### What is gravity?

Gravity is the invisible force of attraction between every bit of matter in the universe. Its strength depends on the mass of the objects involved and just how far they are apart.

### Are mass and weight the same?

No. Mass is the amount of matter in an object. It is the same wherever you measure it. Weight is the force of gravity on an object. It varies with where you measure it.

### Are there other forces?

Wherever there is movement there is a force involved, but there are four basic forces which work right down to the level of atoms. These are gravity, electromagnetism, and two "nuclear" forces—forces that act only in the nuclei of atoms.

Tailwings provide a down force to help keep the car stable

Thrust is developed as hot gas expands between the rocket housing and the air

The shape is smooth and streamlined to cut friction with the air— air resistance

Rocket motors provide huge forward thrust

▲ **Land speed record breaker**
*The main obstacle to traveling fast is friction—friction with the ground, friction with the air, and friction between moving parts. To beat the world land speed record, Thrust II needed huge rocket motors to develop enough thrust to overcome this force.*

### ▶ Strike force

*When a batsman strikes a cricket ball, the ball shoots off somewhere between the direction of the force of the ball's momentum and the direction of the force of the bat. Just where in between depends on the force of the ball's momentum and the force of the strike. The ball's new direction is called the "resultant" by scientists studying forces.*

## What force holds things together?

Nuclear forces hold atomic nuclei together, but electromagnetism holds atoms together, binds atoms to make molecules and binds molecules to make different substances. When it binds molecules, it is called an intermolecular force.

●

## What is friction?

Friction is the force between two things rubbing together, which may be brake pads on a bicycle wheel or air against an airplane. It tends to slow things down, making them hot as momentum is changed to heat. It is caused by the intermolecular force between the molecules of the two things rubbing.

### ▶ Take off

*Airplanes stay up because their wings provide a lift force to counteract the force of gravity. The lift comes from the air that is forced to flow over the wings as the plane flies forward. To take off, the plane must accelerate until it is going fast enough for the wings give the lift to beat gravity.*

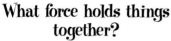

## What is a force field?

A force field is the region over which forces like gravity and electromagnetism have an effect. They are invisible, and the only way of knowing they exist is by the way they move things coming within range. Force fields are often shown as lines with arrows to show the direction and strength of the movement.

●

## How is force measured?

Force is measured in newtons, in honour of Sir Isaac Newton. A newton is the force needed to accelerate 1kg by 1m per second in a second.

# QUIZ

1  What is the force that holds you on the ground?

2  How fast does gravity make things accelerate a) 1 inch (2.5 cm) per second$^2$ b) 32 feet (9.8m) per second$^2$ c) 2,500 miles (4,032km) per second$^2$?

3  What is the force that makes compass needles point North?

4  What force does a train have to overcome to move fast?

5  All forces act in straight lines: true or false?

6  Who dropped different balls from the Leaning Tower of Pisa to show they fall at the same rate?

7  Air resistance gets less the faster a car goes: true or false?

**Answers**
1. Gravity 2. b)
3. Magnetism 4. Friction
5. True
6. Galileo 7. False

# Movement

## How do things start to move?

**T**HINGS ONLY MOVE IF FORCED TO MOVE. This is called inertia. The heavier something is the more inertia it has and the harder it is to start moving. So when something starts to move, there must be a force involved—whether it is visible, like someone pushing, or invisible, like gravity—and the force must be large enough to overcome the inertia. Once things are moving at the same speed and in the same direction, they keep on doing so until another force (typically friction) slows or turns them.

## What's the difference between inertia and momentum?

Inertia is the tendency of things to stay still unless forced to move. Momentum is the tendency of moving things to keep moving, unless forced to stop or slow. This is Newton's First Law of Motion.

●

## What is acceleration?

Acceleration is how fast something gains speed. The larger the force and the lighter the object, the greater the acceleration. This is Newton's Second Law of Motion.

**The four-stroke sequence**

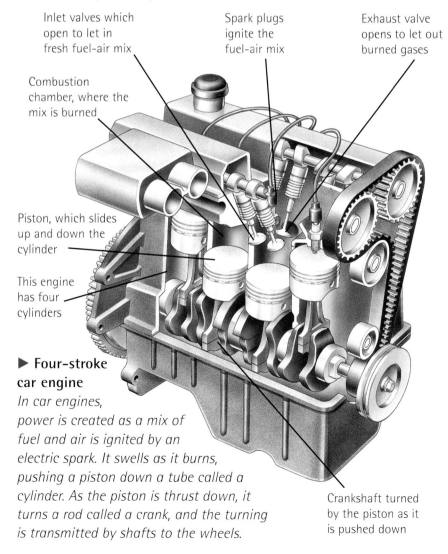

Inlet valves which open to let in fresh fuel-air mix

Spark plugs ignite the fuel-air mix

Exhaust valve opens to let out burned gases

Combustion chamber, where the mix is burned

Piston, which slides up and down the cylinder

This engine has four cylinders

▶ **Four-stroke car engine**
*In car engines, power is created as a mix of fuel and air is ignited by an electric spark. It swells as it burns, pushing a piston down a tube called a cylinder. As the piston is thrust down, it turns a rod called a crank, and the turning is transmitted by shafts to the wheels.*

Crankshaft turned by the piston as it is pushed down

1. Inlet valve opens to let in a dose of fuel drawn in by the descending piston

2. The valve closes and the piston rises, squeezing the fuel as it does

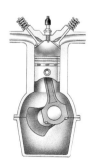

3. The spark ignites the fuel, which swells and thrusts the piston down

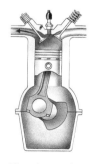

4. The piston rises again, pushing burned gases out of the exhaust

◀ Hydraulic bore
*The arms are raised and lowered on this drill by pumping fluid in and out of the tubes that support them. The drill is driven hydraulically too, to ensure a smooth action.*

## What is Newton's Third Law of Motion?

That for every action, there is an equal and opposite reaction. This means that whenever something moves, there is a balance of forces pushing the other way. So when you push your feet on the bicycle pedals, the pedals are actually pushing back just as hard.

●

## How do engines work?

Most engines work by burning fuel to make gases that expand rapidly as they get hot. In cars and trains, the hot gases swell inside a chamber called the combustion chamber and push against a piston or a turbine (a kind of fan). In jets and rockets, the burning gases swell and push against the whole engine as they shoot out the back.

▶ Jet engine
*A plane's jet engines suck in air through the front to burn with aviation fuel. As it is burned with aviation fuel, it swells so rapidly from the back of the engine that the plane is thrust forward.*

## What is a four-stroke engine?

Most car engines are four-stroke engines. This means that each of the pistons goes up and down four times for each power stroke—that is, for every time the piston is thrust down by the burning gases. Most car engines also have at least four cylinders, and each fires in succession, so that one is on its power stroke while the rest are on their idle strokes.

●

## What is hydraulic power?

Fluids like water cannot be squashed. So if you push fluid through a pipe, it will push out the other end. Hydraulic power uses fluid-filled pipes working like this to drive things smoothly. Hydraulic means water, but most hydraulic systems use oil to avoid rusting.

# QUIZ

1 Why are racing bicycles made of very light materials?

2 How many Laws of Motion did Isaac Newton find?

3 What are the two major fuels used by car engines?

4 What is the gas that combines with fuel as it burns in a car engine?

5 Why do heavy trucks take longer to stop than cars?

6 Which two scientists invented jet engines?

7 What is the force that slows cars down?

8 Cars are powered by dead shellfish: true or false?

9 What is the world's fastest train?

Answers
1. To cut inertia to a minimum 2. Three 3. Gasoline & diesel 4. Oxygen 5. They've more momentum 6. Frank Whittle & Pabst von Ohain. 7. Friction 8. True 9.The French TGV

# Water

## Why is water special?

THERE ARE MANY REASONS why water is a remarkable substance. But there are two that stand out. First of all, it is the only substance that can be solid, liquid, and gas at everyday temperatures. Second, it has a remarkable capacity for making mild solutions with other substances, so that it can be used to transfer everything from sugar to salt. These two properties above all make water perhaps the most important material of all for life–and make Earth, the only planet blessed with an abundance of water, so special.

**▲ Floating ship**
*Ships made of heavy metal float because they trap air inside their hulls. They float at the point where the weight of the ship and air exactly matches the weight of water displaced (pushed out of the way).*

**▼ How submarines work**
*Submarines rise to the surface by pumping water out of their buoyancy tanks to lighten it enough to float to the surface. To dive again, it pumps water into the buoyancy tanks to increase its weight enough to sink.*

### What is water made of?
Water is made of molecules which are built from two atoms of hydrogen and one of oxygen, bound in a Y-shaped. This is why its chemical formula is $H_2O$. This molecule is said to be "polar," because the oxygen side is a little more negatively charged electrically.

### Why is water liquid?
Water is liquid until 212°F (100°C) because its polar molecules form strong bonds with each other, as the positively charged end of one molecule is drawn to the negative end of another. These bonds are called hydrogen bonds.

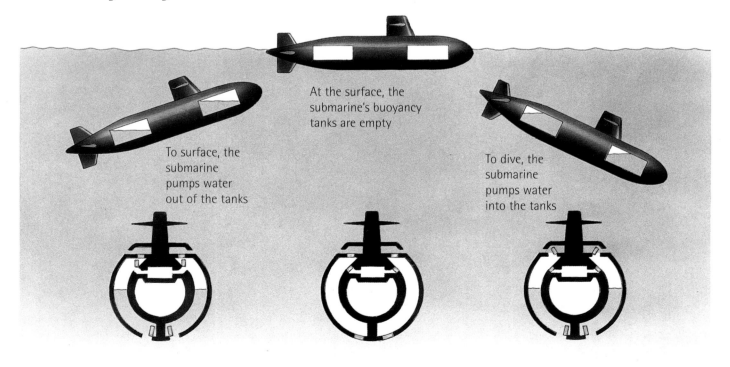

At the surface, the submarine's buoyancy tanks are empty

To surface, the submarine pumps water out of the tanks

To dive, the submarine pumps water into the tanks

# QUIZ

1 So much water flows through the Amazon river that it could fill London's St. Paul's Cathedral in a) 1 second b) 1 minute c) 1 hour ?

2 How much of the world's surface is covered by water: a) 25% b) 55% c) 70%?

3 How much of the world's water is frozen: a) 2% b) 5% c) 12%?

4 Things float better in salty seawater than fresh water: true or false?

5 Which famous scientist shouted 'Eureka!' when he worked out how things float?

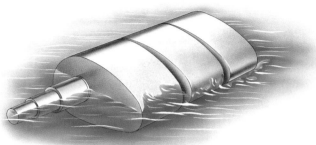

▶ Tidal boom
*The rising and falling of tides in the sea can generate electricity as it waggles floating booms like these to and fro.*

## Why don't lakes freeze solid?

Uniquely, ice is less dense than cold water, so it floats on top, acting as a blanket and stopping cold water below from freezing. Water is at its densest at 39°F (4°C). It actually expands when it freezes, which is why water pipes can burst in cold winters, and how water splits rock.

●

## What is water pressure?

Water pressure is the combined push of moving molecules of water. The deeper the water, the greater the pressure.

## What is a solution?

When a substance is added to a liquid, various things can happen. If the substance does not mix in at all, and lumps of it float in the liquid, it is a "suspension." If the atoms, ions and molecules of the substance break up and intermingle with the liquid it forms a new liquid called a solution. When you dissolve coffee powder in water, you make a solution. Water here is the "solvent" and coffee powder the "solute."

●

## What is a saturated solution?

As you dissolve more of a solid, the solution becomes stronger and stronger until no more will dissolve. The solution is then said to be saturated. If you heat a solution, more will dissolve before it becomes saturated. But if a saturated solution cools down, or is left to evaporate, solute molecules may begin to link and grow into solid crystals.

◀ Sugar solution
*Count how many spoons of sugar you can dissolve in cold water or tea. Then count how many you can dissolve in warm water.*

Answers
1. a) 2. c) 3. a)
4. True
5. The Ancient Greek thinker Archimedes (287–212 BC)

163

# Electricity

## Why does hair go frizzy?

WHEN YOU COMB DRY HAIR tiny electrons are knocked off the atoms in the comb as it rubs past. The effect is that your hair is coated with these tiny negative electrical charges and so is attracted to anything that has the normal amount of electrons, or less. An electrical charge built up like this is called "static" because it does not move. You could try rubbing a balloon on your sweater to create a static charge on the balloon to stick it to a wall.

## What is electric current?

Static electricity does not move. Current electricity does. It is a continuous stream of electrical charge. It only happens when there is a complete, unbroken "circuit" for the current to flow through—typically a loop of copper wire.

## What makes lightning flash?

Lightning flashes produce millions of volts of static electricity. Lightning is created when raindrops and ice crystals inside a thundercloud are flung together by strong air currents. They become electrically charged as they gain or lose electrons. Negatively charged particles build up at the base of the cloud. When this charge has built up enough, it discharges as lightning, either flashing within the cloud or forking between the cloud and ground.

▶ **Lightning flashes**

*Lightning flashes are sparked by the build up of huge differences in static electrical charge between the top and bottom of a thundercloud. The flash is the sudden jump of electrons from one place to another to bring the charge back to normal. This can happen within the cloud (sheet lightning), or between the cloud and ground (fork lightning).*

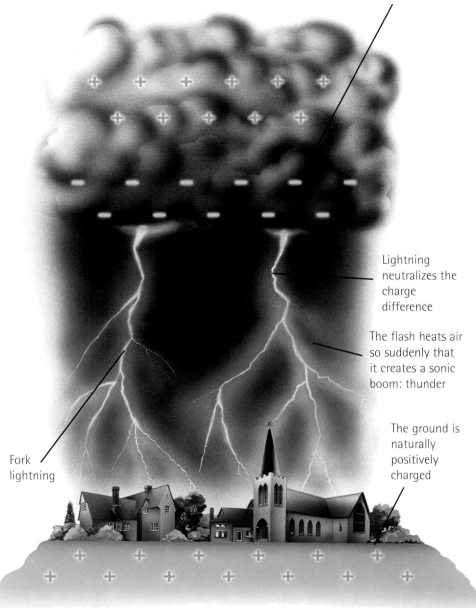

Negative charges build up in the base of the cloud

Lightning neutralizes the charge difference

The flash heats air so suddenly that it creates a sonic boom: thunder

The ground is naturally positively charged

Fork lightning

# QUIZ

**▲ Simple battery**
*Acid contains both positive and negative particles. When copper and zinc plates are dipped in and connected, pluses are drawn to one, minuses to the other.*

## How does current flow?
The charge in an electric current is electrons that have broken free from their atoms. None of them moves very far, but the current is passed on as they bang into each other like rows of marbles.

## How do batteries work?
Batteries work because when certain substances are placed next to each other, there is a difference in charge between them. In the simplest cells, the materials are copper and zinc plates dipped in acid. When a wire between the plates completes the circuit, current flows.

**▶ Flashlight**
*In a flashlight the electrical power comes from the charge difference between chemicals in the batteries—typically zinc and carbon. One end of the batteries touches the casing. The other touches the bulb to complete the circuit. The bulb glows because the current meets resistance in the bulb's thin filament.*

**▲ Electric current**
*Electric current in a wire is passed on by free electrons (tiny blue dots). The electrons are drawn to the positive nuclei of atoms (red).*

## What is resistance?
Not all substances conduct electric currents equally well. Resistance is a substance's tendency to block the flow of current. A narrow place in the circuit can also be a resistance and the wire here can get very hot. In light bulbs, a thin section of wire or "filament" is what glows. A fuse is a thin bit of wire that burns through and breaks the circuit if it gets overloaded.

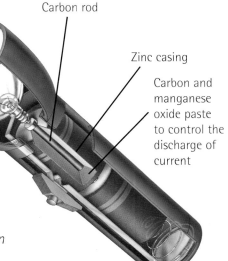

Carbon rod

Zinc casing

Carbon and manganese oxide paste to control the discharge of current

1 The electric current that supplies your house switches direction several times a second: true or false?

2 What two metals are the best conductors of electricity?

3 A volt is a measure of
a) electrical resistance
b) a difference in charge
c) the speed of the current

4 Who invented the battery
a) Volta b) Faraday
c) Maxwell?

5 Which American statesman discovered the electrical nature of lightning?

6 A battery that uses paste rather than acid is called a dry cell: true or false?

7 A good place to stand in a thunderstorm is under a tall tree: true or false?

8 Who discovered the link between electricity and magnetism?

Answers
1. True 2. Copper and silver 3. b) 4. a) 5. Benjamin Franklin 6. True 7. False; trees attract lightning 8. Michael Faraday

# Electronics

## What are electronics?

ELECTRONICS ARE SYSTEMS that control things by switching on and off tiny electrical circuits. The switches are not like light switches on the wall, but work automatically. The simplest are transistors; the most complex are linked together in integrated circuits, silicon chips and microprocessors. These are the clever systems that control everything from cookers to guided missiles.

**▲ Aircraft flight deck**
*The flight deck of a modern aircraft flight deck is almost entirely "glass," which means it is full of electronic control screens and displays.*

### How do electronic systems work?

Inside every electronic device, from TVs to air traffic control systems, there are scores or even millions of tiny electric circuits continually switching on and off. The operation of the device depends on which circuits are on and which are off. In a computer, each bit of data is directed through a different combination of circuits.

●

### What are transistors?

Transistors are tiny switches made from materials called semiconductors, including germanium and silicon. What makes them special is that their ability to conduct electricity changes quickly as they warm up. Transistors can be used to control an electric current in several ways, including amplifying it (making it bigger) and switching it on and off.

### What is a silicon chip?

Dozens or even thousands of tiny transistors can be joined together in a single "integrated circuit." This can be printed onto a tiny sliver of silicon, called a silicon chip. They can be anything from simple circuits for a clock to complex microprocessors for controlling computers.

Internet   Computer   Radio mast   Radio   Satellite dish

  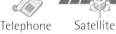

TV   Telephone   Satellite

### What are bits in computers?

Since electronic circuits can only be on or off, computers work by using a "binary" system. This codes all data as either 1s or 0s, "ons" or "offs." Each is called a "bit," and bits are grouped together in bytes. This is why a computer's ability to handle data is measured in bytes.

## How do computers remember?

Some computer memory is printed into microcircuits when it is made. This is ROM (Read-only memory). RAM (Random-access memory) circuits take new data and instructions. Data is also stored in magnetic patterns on removable discs or in the laser-guided bumps on CDs.

## What is a fractal?

In improving computers, scientists have learned much about numbers. Fractals are beautiful patterns generated by the computer from simple repeated mathematical calculations. Since they seem to mimic natural shapes like trees, some believe such shapes were created in a similar way, step by step.

## What is virtual reality?

Virtual reality (VR) systems build a picture electronically to give you the illusion of reality. Special eyepieces show a slightly different view to each eye, giving the impression of a real, 3D space. As the view in each changes, it seems you are moving through a real space. Special gloves and other devices to control movement enhance the illusion. VR devices are now used for a wide range of tasks, as well as games. With VR, people can operate a computer-guided device in places where it is far too dangerous or difficult to work themselves, including in wrecks under the sea, inside the body and many other places.

▼ **Telecommunications**
*The telecommunications systems that now allow virtually instant communication around the world would not be possible without tiny electronic control devices and circuits.*

# QUIZ

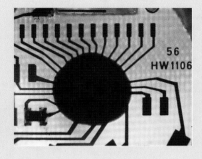

1 **What does CAD stand for: a) Computer-aided Design b) Calculating Arithmetical Device c) Continually-activated Diode?**

2 **The first computer was built by Charles Babbage in the 1830s: true or false?**

3 **Electronic devices can be grown by bacteria: true or false?**

4 **The internet was first developed by the American military: true or false?**

5 **What is the artificial environment created by computers called?**

6 **Robot is a Czech word for forced labour: true or false?**

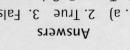

**Answers**
1. a) 2. True 3. False
4. True 5. Cyberspace
6. True

# Light

## What is light?

LIGHT IS WHAT YOU SEE THINGS BY. It is a radiation sent out by atoms in light sources such as the sun, stars, and electric lights. There are other kinds of radiation, but light is the only kind your eyes can see. Light always moves in straight lines, and so people talk about light rays, but rays are just the straight path taken by the light.

### ▲ Splitting colors
*Daylight and most other lights contain a whole mixture of different wavelengths—different colors—of light. Daylight can be split into a full range of colors, or spectrum, with a triangular chunk of glass called a prism. The prism bends each color of light to a different extent, so each emerges from the prism in a different place.*

### ▼ Electromagnetic spectrum
*Light is just a small part of a huge range of radiation sent out by atoms. At one end are radio waves and microwaves, and infrared heat radiation. At the other are ultraviolet light (which we can't see), and X-rays and gamma rays.*

### Does light travel in waves?
In the last century, most scientists thought light did travel in tiny waves fractions of a millimeter long, rather than in bulletlike particles. Now they agree it can be both, and it is best to think of light as vibrating packets of energy.

### What are photons?
Photons are almost infinitessimally small particles of light They have no mass and there are billions of them in a single light beam.

### What is a shadow?
Since light travels in straight lines, its path is blocked whenever it meets an obstacle. The shadow is the dark space behind the obstacle.

### What happens when light hits things?
When light rays hit a surface, some bounce off. This is called reflection. Some are absorbed by atoms in the surface, warming it very slightly. If the surface is transparent, like glass, some will pass straight through.

### Does light change when it hits a surface?
Each kind of atom absorbs a particular wavelength (color) of light. The color of a surface depends on the atoms it contains and so which wavelengths are absorbed and which reflected. A leaf is green because the leaf's atoms soak up all colors but green from sunlight, and you see only the reflected green light.

| Radio waves | Microwaves | Infrared | Visible light |
| --- | --- | --- | --- |

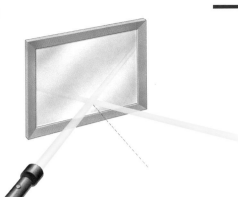

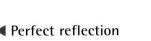

**◄ Perfect reflection**
*Mirrors give a clear reflection because light bounces off them at exactly the same angle that it hits them.*

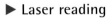

**▶ Laser reading**
*The perfect precision of laser light means it can be used to pick up the tiny pits on the surface of a CD that store the memory of the music. The laser light is bounced into them and the head picks up the reflections from the pits.*

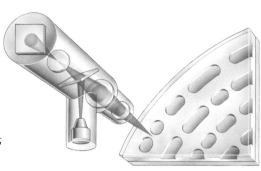

## How is light bent?

The bending of light rays is called refraction. This happens when they strike a transparent material like glass or water at an angle. The different materials slow the light waves down, so that they bend around, like car wheels driving onto sand.

## How do mirrors work?

Most mirrors are made of glass, but the back is coated with a shiny metal (called silvering) that perfectly reflects all the light that hits it, at exactly the same angle.

## Why is laser light special?

Most light contains a jumbled mix of different wavelengths. Laser light contains only a single wavelength— and what's more, all the waves are traveling perfectly in step. This means the beam can deliver a very concentrated but small burst of energy.

## How do fiber-optics bend light?

They don't; they simply bounce it again and again down the shiny insides of the long, thin glass fibers they are made from.

# QUIZ

1  A frosted glass window is
a) opaque b) transparent
c) translucent?

2  Where do the colours of the rainbow come from?

3  Many birds can see ultraviolet light: true or false?

4  The angle that light strikes a mirror is called
a) the angle of reflection
b) the angle of incidence
c) the light angle?

5  Things are the same colour in the dark as they are in daylight: true or false?

6  A light bulb works because the pressure of the electric current through its thin filament makes it glow: true or false?

Ultraviolet        X-rays          Gamma rays

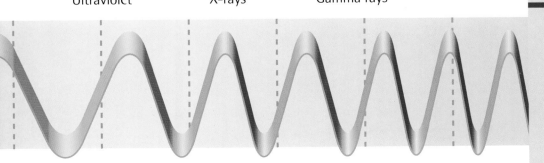

6. True
colour at all in the dark
4. b)  5. False; they have no
1. c)  2. Sunlight  3. True
**Answers**

# Sound

## What is sound?

SOUND IS VIBRATIONS IN THE AIR. Sometimes you can see the vibration; sometimes you cannot. If you pluck a taut rubber band, you can see the band twang. If you clap your hands, you see nothing. Vibration is there all the same. But it is not only the band or your hands that move. You hear the sound because the air moves too. As the source of the sound moves, it sets the air molecules moving to, and so the vibration is transmitted through the air to your ears.

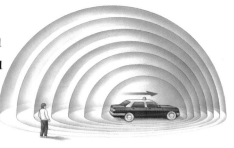

▲ Doppler effect
*The sound of a car's engine drops in pitch as it zooms away from you because the sound waves are stretched out behind it.*

### Can sound travel in a vacuum?

No. Sound can travel through solids and liquids as well as air. In fact, it can travel faster through solids and liquids than air, because their molecules are more closely packed. But there is always complete silence in a vacuum because there is nothing to vibrate.

### What are sound waves?

Sound waves are not like waves in the sea, which go up and down. Sound waves move by alternately stretching and squeezing. When a sound is made, air molecules near the sound are squeezed together. They, in turn, jostle up against the molecules next to them—and then are pulled back into place by the molecules behind.

### How do you hear sounds?

You hear because your ears pick up the tiny vibrations in the air made by sounds. Inside the ear is a taut, thin window of skin called the eardrum, which vibrates with the air and rattles three tiny bones called ossicles. The last of them, called the stirrup, rattles farther than the first and amplifies the sound. The stirrup shakes another thin skin, sending waves through a fluid filled tube called the cochlea, deep inside your head. Ripples in the cochlea trigger sensitive nerve receptors to send signals to your brain.

### What is an echo?

An echo is sound bouncing back. You don't often hear echoes, because sound only bounces back clearly off smooth, hard surfaces, and in confined spaces. Even in a confined space, the wall must be at least 56 feet (17m) away— which is why you usually hear echoes only in large empty halls.

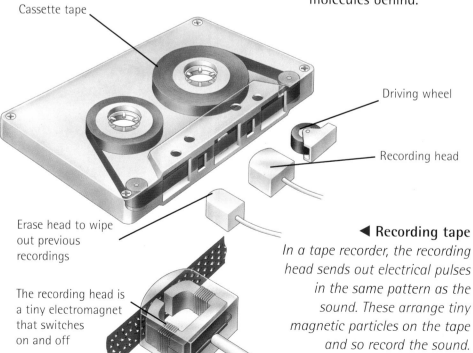

Cassette tape

Driving wheel

Recording head

Erase head to wipe out previous recordings

The recording head is a tiny electromagnet that switches on and off

◀ Recording tape
*In a tape recorder, the recording head sends out electrical pulses in the same pattern as the sound. These arrange tiny magnetic particles on the tape and so record the sound.*

# QUIZ

1 What is the study of the way sound behaves called?

2 What scale is the loudness of a sound measured on?

3 The highest frequency a human can hear is
a) 5,000 Hz b) 20,000 Hz c) 50,000 Hz?

4 Which does sound travel fastest in: a) air b) water c) metal?

5 The longest strings in a piano produce the highest notes: true or false?

6 Ultrasound is sounds too high for humans to hear: true or false?

7 Bats locate prey in the dark by sending out beams of ultrasound: true or false?

### ▼ The sound barrier

*The sound barrier was broken for the first time in 1947 by American test pilot, Chuck Yeager flying the specially built Bell X-1.*

### What is the sound barrier?

When a plane starts to fly faster than sound, it breaks the sound barrier. There is no real barrier to break. But as the aircraft travels faster and faster it squashes the air in front of it, generating a shock wave that is heard as a loud explosive sound called a sonic boom.

### What is sound frequency?

Some sounds like squealing brakes are high-pitched. Others like thunder, are low-pitched. The difference is in how frequently the sound waves follow each other. If the waves come in quick succession, the sound is high-pitched. If they are widely separated, the sound is low-pitched. A low sound is 20 Hz, or waves per second. A high sound is 20,000 Hz.

### What's the speed of sound?

In air, sound travels about 1,115 feet (340m) per second. It travels faster on a hot day.

### ▶ Squeezing the air

*When a loudspeaker vibrates with a sound, the vibrations travel out through the air in a series of waves that alternately squeeze the air molecules together and stretch them apart.*

**Answers**
1. Acoustics 2. Decibel 3. b) 4. metal 5. False 6. True 7. True

171

# Magnetism

## What is magnetism?

**M**AGNETISM IS AN INVISIBLE FORCE, which acts between iron, steel, and a few other metals. Each magnet has an area around it where it exerts its force power, called its magnetic field. This field gets weaker farther away from the magnet. But if another magnetic material comes closer, the magnet either pulls it closer or pushes it away.

### What is a magnetic pole?

Magnetic force is especially strong at the end of each magnet. These two ends are called the poles. One is called the north (or north-seeking) pole, because if the magnet is suspended freely, this pole swings round until it points north. The other is called the south pole. If the opposite poles of two magnets come close, they will be drawn together. If the same poles meet, they will push each other apart.

### What is a lodestone?

Long before people learned how to make steel magnets, they found that certain rocks attract or repel each other, and bits of iron. These rocks are called lodestones, and contain iron oxide, which makes them naturally magnetic.

▶ **Magnetic field**

*This illustration shows the magnetic field around a simple bar magnet. The lines indicate the direction in which the force works—from turning magnetic materials toward its poles.*

### Why is the Earth magnetic?

As the Earth spins, the swirling of its iron nickel core turns it into a giant magnet. Like a bar magnet, Earth has two poles, North and South. It is because the Earth is a magnet that small magnets point the same way if left to swivel freely.

### How big is Earth's field?

Earth's magnetic field extends far out into space, forming a plum-shaped barrier called the magnetosphere. On the side facing the Sun it stretches out 37,000 miles (60,000km). On the far side it is blown out four times this far by the solar wind.

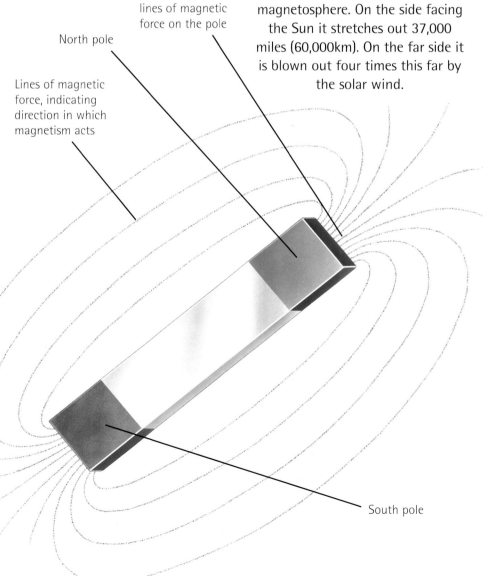

Concentration of lines of magnetic force on the pole

North pole

Lines of magnetic force, indicating direction in which magnetism acts

South pole

172

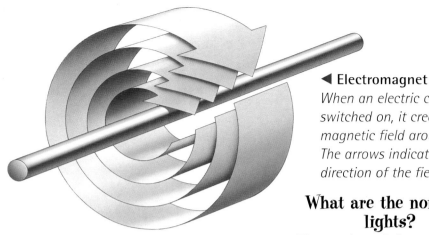

◀ **Electromagnet**

*When an electric current is switched on, it creates a magnetic field around the wire. The arrows indicate the direction of the field.*

## What is electromagnetism?

Electricity and magnetism are deeply linked. Every electric current creates a magnetic field around it, and moving a magnet past an electric wire will induce (create) an electric current in it. An electromagnet is a coil of copper wire, which creates a very strong magnetic field when a current is switched through it.

## What are the northern lights?

The northern lights, or Aurora Borealis, are spectacular curtains of light that shimmer in the night sky over the North pole. They occur because there is a cleft in the magnetosphere above the pole, where lines of magnetic force funnel in. Every now and then, charged particles from the Sun stream in here and cannon into air molecules, making them glow brightly.

▼ **The Northern Lights**

*The interaction of solar radiation with the Earth's magnetic field creates spectacular light shows or auroras over the North and South Poles.*

# QUIZ

1 What did sailors use magnets for?

2 Iron loses its magnetism above 1400°F: true or false?

3 Every magnet has two poles, no matter what its shape: true or false?

4 The effects of magnetic attraction are not transmitted between objects: true or false?

5 Aluminium is magnetic: true or false?

6 The Earth's magnetic North Pole is hundreds of miles from the North Pole: true or false?

7 What is the aurora over the South Pole called?

173

# Nuclear power

## Why is nuclear power huge?

THE ENERGY THAT BINDS TOGETHER the nucleus of an atom is huge, even though the nucleus is minute. In fact, as Einstein showed in 1905 with his theory of Special Relativity, the particles of the atom can be regarded as pure energy. It is releasing some of this energy from millions of atomic nuclei that allow nuclear power stations to generate so much power from just a few tons of nuclear fuel. It also gives nuclear bombs their terrifying destructive power.

### What is nuclear fusion?
Nuclear fusion is when nuclear energy is released by fusing or joining together small atoms like those of deuterium (a form of hydrogen). Nuclear fusion is the reaction that keeps stars glowing and provides the energy for H-bombs (see *What is an atomic bomb?*) Scientists hope to find a way of harnessing it for power.

▼ A nuclear power station

*Inside a nuclear reactor there are fuel rods made from pellets of uranium oxide, separated by spacers. When the station goes on-line, a nuclear fission chain reaction is set up in the fuel rods. This is slowed down by control rods, which absorb the neutrons so that heat is produced steadily to make the steam that drives the turbines that generate electricity.*

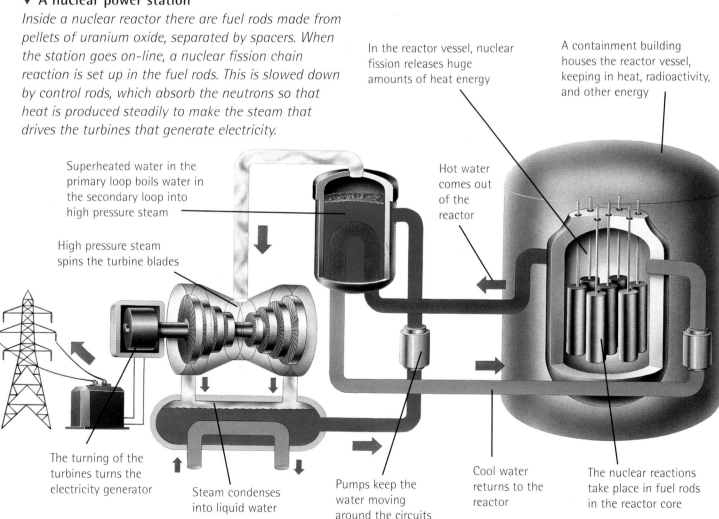

In the reactor vessel, nuclear fission releases huge amounts of heat energy

A containment building houses the reactor vessel, keeping in heat, radioactivity, and other energy

Superheated water in the primary loop boils water in the secondary loop into high pressure steam

Hot water comes out of the reactor

High pressure steam spins the turbine blades

The turning of the turbines turns the electricity generator

Steam condenses into liquid water

Pumps keep the water moving around the circuits

Cool water returns to the reactor

The nuclear reactions take place in fuel rods in the reactor core

▶ **Nuclear fission**
*Nuclear fission involves firing a neutron (yellow ball) at a nucleus of uranium or plutonium. When the nuclei splits, it fires out more neutrons, which split more nuclei, creating a chain reaction.*

### What is nuclear fission?
Nuclear fission releases energy by splitting large nuclei such as uranium and plutonium. To split the nuclei, neutrons are fired at it. As they crash into it, they split off more neutrons, which bombard other nuclei, setting off a chain reaction.

### What is an atomic bomb?
An atomic bomb or A-bomb is one of the two main kinds of nuclear weapon. An A-bomb relies on the explosive nuclear fission of uranium-235 or plutonium-239. Hydrogen bombs, also called H-bombs or thermonuclear weapons, rely on the fusion of hydrogen atoms to create explosions a thousand times bigger.

### Who invented the A-bomb?
The first A-bombs were developed in the USA toward the end of World War II by a team led by Robert Oppenheimer (1904-1967). Their first bombs were dropped on Hiroshima and Nagasaki in Japan in 1945 with devastating effect.

### What is radioactivity?
The atoms of an element often come in several different forms or isotopes. Each form has a different number of neutrons in its nucleus, indicated in the name, as in carbon-12 and carbon-14. The nuclei of some of these isotopes— the ones scientists call radioisotopes—are unstable, and decay (break up). As they break up, they release radiation, consisting of streams of particles called alpha, beta, and gamma rays. This is radioactivity.

### What is half-life?
No one can predict when the atomic nucleus will decay. But scientists can predict how long it will take for half the particles in a substance to decay. This is its half-life. Strontium-90 has a half-life of just nine minutes. Uranium-235, on the other hand, has a half-life of four and a half billion years. Most fall somewhere in between.

# QUIZ

1  Exposure to high levels of radioactivity can be fatal: true or false?

2  Which two countries have the biggest stockpile of nuclear weapons?

3  Nuclear power stations do not burn fuel: true or false?

4  Where in the Ukraine was there a major accident at a nuclear power station?

5  What is the most devastating accident that can happen to a nuclear reactor?

6  The age of many ancient remains can be dated by their radioactivity: true or false?

7  What do the stars and H-bombs have in common?

**Answers**
1. True  2. The USA and the Russian Federation  3. False  4. Chernobyl  5. Meltdown  6. True  7. Nuclear fusion

# Amazing answers

## Highest waterfalls

| | |
|---|---|
| Angel Falls (Venezuela) | 3,212ft |
| Yosemite Falls (USA) | 2,425ft |
| Mardalsfossen (S)(Norway) | 2,425ft |
| Tugela Falls (S. Africa) | 2,011ft |
| Cuquenan Falls (Venez.) | 2,001ft |
| Sutherland Falls (NZ) | 1.903ft |
| Ribbon Falls (USA) | 1,611ft |
| Great Falls (Guyana) | 1,601ft |
| Mardalsfossen (N) | 1,536ft |
| Della Falls (Canada) | 1,444ft |
| Gavarnie Falls (France) | 1,385ft |
| Skjeggedal Falls (N'way) | 1,378ft |
| Glass Falls (Brazil) | 1,326ft |
| Krimml Falls (Austria) | 1,312ft |
| Trummelbach Falls (Switz) | 1,312ft |
| Takakkaw Falls (Canada) | 1,201ft |
| Silver Strand Falls (USA) | 1,171ft |
| Wallaman Falls (Aus) | 1,138ft |

## Cities

**The world's biggest cities**

| | |
|---|---|
| Mexico City | 14,987,051 |
| Cairo | 13,000,000 |
| Shangai | 12,760,000 |
| Bombay | 12,571,720 |
| Tokyo | 11,718,720 |
| Seoul | 10,920,000 |
| Calcutta | 10,916,272 |
| Beijing | 10,860,000 |
| São Paulo | 9,480,427 |
| Paris | 9,318,800 |
| Moscow | 8,700,000 |
| Delhi | 8,375,188 |
| Jakarta | 7,885,519 |
| New York | 7,322,564 |
| Istanbul | 7,309,190 |
| Karachi | 7,183,000 |
| London | 6,934,500 |

## Populations

**The most populous countries**

| | |
|---|---|
| China | 1,188,000,000 |
| India | 879,500,000 |
| USA | 255,200,000 |
| Indonesia | 191,200,000 |
| Brazil | 154,100,000 |
| Russia | 149,003,000 |
| Pakistan | 124,800,000 |
| Japan | 124,500,000 |
| Bangladesh | 119,300,000 |
| Nigeria | 115,700,000 |
| Mexico | 88,200,000 |
| Germany | 80,300,000 |
| Vietnam | 69,500,000 |
| Philippines | 65,200,000 |
| Iran | 61,600,000 |
| Turkey | 58,400,000 |
| Italy | 57,800,000 |
| United Kingdom | 57,700,000 |
| France | 57,200,000 |
| Thailand | 56,100,000 |
| Egypt | 54,800,000 |

**The least populous countries**

| | |
|---|---|
| Vatican City | 1,000 |
| Nauru | 9,000 |
| Tuvalu | 9,000 |
| Belau | 15,100 |
| San Marino | 23,000 |
| Monaco | 28,000 |

# Biggest lakes

| | | | |
|---|---|---|---|
| Caspian Sea | 143,203 sq mi | Lake Ontario | 7,334 sq mi |
| Lake Superior | 32,518 sq mi | Lake Balkhash | 7,113 sq mi |
| Lake Victoria | 26,813 sq mi | Lake Ladoga | 6,833 sq mi |
| Aral Sea | 24,897 sq mi | Lake Chad | 6,298 sq mi |
| Lake Huron | 24,355 sq mi | Lake Maracaibo | 5,119 sq mi |
| Lake Michigan | 22,294 sq mi | Patos | 3,919 sq mi |
| Lake Tanganyika | 12,647 sq mi | Lake Onega | 3,709 sq mi |
| Lake Baikal | 12,157 sq mi | Lake Eyre | 3,598 sq mi |
| Great Bear Lake | 12,093 sq mi | Lake Titicaca | 3,199 sq mi |
| Lake Nyasa | 11,147 sq mi | Lake Nicaragua | 3,099 sq mi |
| Great Slave Lake | 11,027 sq mi | Lake Mai-Ndombe | 3,099 sq mi |
| Lake Erie | 9,963 sq mi | Lake Athabasca | 3,063 sq mi |
| Lake Winnipeg | 9,413 sq mi | | |

# Richest and poorest

| The world's richest countries GNP per head in the 90s $US | | The world's poorest countries GNP per head in the 90s | |
|---|---|---|---|
| Switzerland | 33,510 | Mozambique | 60 |
| Liechtenstein | 33,000 | Tanzania | 110 |
| Luxembourg | 31,080 | Ethiopia | 110 |
| Japan | 26,920 | Somalia | 150 |
| Sweden | 25,490 | Nepal | 170 |
| Finland | 24,400 | Sierra Leone | 170 |
| Norway | 24,160 | Uganda | 170 |
| Denmark | 23,660 | Bhutan | 180 |
| Germany | 23,650 | Cambodia | 200 |
| Iceland | 22,580 | Guinea-Bissau | 210 |
| USA | 22,560 | Burundi | 210 |
| Canada | 21,260 | Malawi | 210 |
| France | 20,600 | Bangladesh | 220 |
| Austria | 20,380 | Chad | 220 |
| | | Zaïre | 220 |

# Mountains

**The world's highest mountains**

*Asia*

| | |
|---|---|
| Everest | 29,030ft |
| K2 | 28,253ft |
| Kanchenjunga | 28,210ft |

*South America*

| | |
|---|---|
| Aconcagua | 22,836ft |
| Ojos del Salado | 22,665ft |
| Bonete | 22,547ft |

*North America*

| | |
|---|---|
| McKinley | 20,323ft |
| Logan | 19,525ft |
| Citlaltépetl | 18,406ft |

*Africa*

| | |
|---|---|
| Kilimanjaro | 19,341ft |
| Kenya | 17,061ft |
| Margherita Peak | 16,763ft |

*Europe*

| | |
|---|---|
| Elbrus | 18,511ft |
| Dykh Tau | 17,071ft |
| Shkara | 17,064ft |

*Oceania*

| | |
|---|---|
| Wilhelm | 14,794ft |
| Cook | 12,317ft |
| Tasman | 11,474ft |

# Amazing answers

## The Earth's dimensions

Circumference at the equator
24,902mi
Circumference at the poles
24,860mi
Diameter at the equator
7,926mi
Diameter at the poles
7,900mi
Land surface
57,491,000 sq mi
Water surface
525,397,000 sq mi
Surface area
196,888,000 sq mi
Mean distance from the Sun
92,898,000 mi
Average speed around the Sun
19mi /sec

## Continents

**Asia**
Area                17,119,000 sq mi
Population          3,112,700,000
Population density
(People per sq mi)          293

**Africa**
Area                11,696,000 sq mi
Population          642,111,000
Population density          54

**North America**
Area                9,560,000 sq mi
Population          427,226,000
Population density          34

**South America**
Area                6,870,000 sq mi
Population          296,716,000
Population density          44

**Europe**
Area                4,053,000 sq mi
Population          498,371,000
Population density          249

**Oceania**
Area                3,281,000 sq mi
Population          26,481,000
Population density          8

**Antarctica**
Area                5,500,000 sq mi

## Glaciers

**The world's longest glaciers**

Lambert-Fisher Ice Passage
(Antarctica)          320mi
Petermanns Glacier
(Greenland)          125mi
Hubbard Glacier
(N.America)          80mi
Siachen Glacier
(Karakoram, Asia)          47mi
Skeidarajokull
(Iceland)          30mi
Tasman
(New Zealand)          18mi
Aletsch Gletscher
(European Alps)          15mi

# Biggest and smallest countries

| The world's biggest countries | | The world's smallest countries | |
| --- | --- | --- | --- |
| Russia | 6,591,104 sq mi | Vatican City | 0.15 sq mi |
| Canada | 3,848,655 sq mi | Monaco | 0.75 sq mi |
| China | 3,694,521 sq mi | Nauru | 2 sq mi |
| USA | 3,617,829 sq mi | Tuvalu | 10 sq mi |
| Brazil | 3,285,618 sq mi | San Marino | 24 sq mi |
| Australia | 2,965,368 sq mi | Liechtenstein | 62 sq mi |
| India | 1,229,417 sq mi | Marshall Islands | 70 sq mi |
| Argentina | 1,073,115 sq mi | St Kitts & Nevis | 101 sq mi |
| Kazakhstan | 1,048,877 sq mi | Maldives | 115 sq mi |
| Sudan | 967,316 sq mi | Malta | 122 sq mi |
| Algeria | 919,352 sq mi | Grenada | 133 sq mi |
| Zaïre | 904,764 sq mi | St Vincent | 150 sq mi |
| Saudi Arabia | 829,780 sq mi | Barbados | 166 sq mi |
| Mexico | 755,865 sq mi | Antigua & Barbuda | 171 sq mi |
| Indonesia | 735,163 sq mi | Andorra | 181 sq mi |
| Libya | 685,343 sq mi | Seychelles | 185 sq mi |
| Iran | 636,128 sq mi | Belau | 196 sq mi |
| Mongolia | 604,090 sq mi | St Lucia | 238 sq mi |
| Peru | 496,093 sq mi | Singapore | 239 sq mi |
| Chad | 495,624 sq mi | Bahrain | 240 sq mi |

# Weather

**The world's sunniest place**
The Eastern Sahara, which has sunshine for more than 90% of all daylight hours.

**The world's hottest place**
Dallol in Ethiopia, where the average temperature is 93°f in the shade.

**The world's driest place**
The Atacama Desert in Chile, with an annual average of just 0.02in of rain.

**The world's coldest place**
Vostok in Antarctica, where it averages -72°f.

# Major deserts of the world

| | | | |
| --- | --- | --- | --- |
| Sahara | 3,506,800 sq mi | Great Victoria | 130,700 sq mi |
| Arabian | 899,400 sq mi | Gibson | 120,000 sq mi |
| Gobi | 499,900 sq mi | Thar | 100,000 sq mi |
| Patagonian | 259,800 sq mi | Atacama | 70,000 sq mi |
| Rub al-Khali | 250,000 sq mi | Sonoran | 70,000 sq mi |
| Kalahari | 204,000 sq mi | Simpson | 40,000 sq mi |
| Chihuahuan | 173,700 sq mi | An Nafud | 40,000 sq mi |
| Taklimakan | 140,600 sq mi | Mojave | 15,000 sq mi |
| Kara Kum | 135,700 sq mi | Death Valley | 3,000 sq mi |
| Great Sandy | 130,700 sq mi | Namib | 500 sq mi |

# Amazing answers

##  Major rivers of the world

|  |  |  |  |
|---|---|---|---|
| | | Amur-Shilka | 2,744mi |
| | | Lena | 2,734mi |
| | | Congo | 2,718mi |
| | | Mackenzie-Peace-Finlay | 2,635mi |
| | | Mekong | 2,597mi |
| | | Missouri-Red Rock | 2,563mi |
| | | Niger | 2,548mi |
| | | Plate-Parana | 2,450mi |
| Nile | 4,147mi | Mississippi | 2,348mi |
| Amazon | 4,083mi | Murray-Darling | 2,331mi |
| Yangtze | 3,900mi | Missouri | 2,315mi |
| Mississippi-Missouri-Red Rock | 3,740mi | Volga | 2,194mi |
| Ob-Irtysh | 3,362mi | Madeira | 2,014mi |
| Yenesei-Angara | 3,100mi | Purus | 1,995mi |
| Yellow | 2,877mi | São Fransisco | 1,989mi |
| | | Yukon | 1,979mi |

|  |  |
|---|---|
| St Lawrence | 1,900mi |
| Rio Grande | 1,833mi |
| Tunguska, Lower | 1,861mi |
| Indus | 1,800mi |
| Danube | 1,775mi |
| Salween | 1,770mi |
| Brahmaputra | 1,700mi |
| Euphrates | 1,700mi |
| Para-Tocantins | 1,677mi |
| Zambezi | 1,600mi |
| Nelson-S.Saskatchewan-Bow | 1,600mi |
| Paraguay | 1,584mi |
| Amu Darya | 1,579mi |
| Kolyma | 1,562mi |
| Ganges | 1,550mi |
| Ural | 1,509mi |

##  Islands

### The world's biggest islands

| | sq mi |
|---|---|
| Greenland | 839,782 |
| New Guinea | 304,921 |
| Borneo | 289,925 |
| Madagascar | 226,598 |
| Baffin (Canada) | 195,876 |
| Sumatra (Indonesia) | 163,957 |
| Honshu, Japan | 87,782 |
| Great Britain | 84,178 |
| Victoria, (Can) | 83,874 |
| Ellesmere (Can) | 75,747 |
| Sulawesi (Indo) | 73,037 |
| South Island (NZ) | 58,369 |
| Java (Indo) | 48,829 |

##  Earthquake disasters

| Date | Location | death toll |
|---|---|---|
| 464BC | Sparta, Greece | 20,000 |
| 856AD | Corinth, Greece | 45,000 |
| 856 | Damghan, Iran | 200,000 |
| 893 | Ardabil, Iran | 150,000 |
| 1038 | Chihli, China | 100,000 |
| 1138 | Aleppo, Syria | 230,000 |
| 1293 | Kamekura, Japan | 30,000 |
| 1556 | Shansi, China | 800,000 |
| 1667 | Shemaka, the Caucasus | 80,000 |
| 1731 | Peking, China | 100,000 |
| 1737 | Calcutta, India | 300,000 |
| 1755 | Lisbon, Portugal | 100,000 |

| Date | Location | death toll |
|---|---|---|
| 1906 | San Fransisco, US | 3,000 |
| 1908 | Messina, Italy | 160,000 |
| 1920 | Kanshu, China | 200,000 |
| 1923 | Kwanto, Japan | 144,000 |
| 1960 | Southern Chile | 5,700 |
| 1964 | Anchorage, Alaska | 131 |
| 1970 | Ancash, Peru | 66,000 |
| 1976 | Tangshan, China | 655,000 |
| 1985 | Michoacán, Mexico | 9,500 |
| 1994 | Northridge, US | 60 |
| 1995 | Kobe, Japan | 5,200 |

# Caves

### The biggest cave chamber
The Sarawak Chamber in Malaysia, with an area of 1,751,303 sq ft, length of 2,300ft, and average width of 985ft. The roof is 230ft high at its lowest point.

### The longest stalactite
20.35ft, in the Poll an Ionana cave, County Clare, Ireland.

### The tallest stalagmite
105ft, in the Krásnohorska cave in the Czech Republic.

# Sea deeps

### The deepest sea trenches

|                     | feet from sea level |
| ------------------- | ------------------- |
| Mariana             | 35,829              |
| Tonga               | 35,435              |
| Philippine          | 32,997              |
| Kermadec            | 32,964              |
| Izu-Ogasawara       | 32,088              |
| Kuril               | 31,334              |
| North New Hebrides  | 30,103              |
| New Britain         | 29,332              |
| Puerto Rico         | 28,233              |
| Yap                 | 27,977              |

# Oceans

### Oceans

| Pacific  | 62,628 sq mi |
| -------- | ------------ |
| Atlantic | 31,822 sq mi |
| Indian   | 28,348 sq mi |
| Arctic   | 5,439 sq mi  |

### Seas

| South China     | 1,342 sq mi |
| --------------- | ----------- |
| Caribbean       | 1,063 sq mi |
| Mediterranean   | 967 sq mi   |
| Gulf of Mexico  | 596 sq mi   |
| Sea of Japan    | 389 sq mi   |
| East China      | 290 sq mi   |
| North           | 222 sq mi   |
| Black           | 178 sq mi   |
| Baltic          | 163 sq mi   |

# Amazing volcanoes

### The biggest eruptions
• Tamboro, Indonesia, 1815
19 cubic mi of ash emitted.
• Krakatoa, Indonesia, 1883
4 cubic mi of ash emitted.
• Katmai, Alaska, 1912
3 cubic mi of ash emitted
• Pinatubo, Philippines, 1991
1.7 cubic mi of ash emitted
• Vesuvius, Italy, 79AD
0.75 cubic mi of ash emitted.
• St Helens, USA, 1980
0.25 cubic mi of ash emitted.

### The largest active volcano
Mauna Loa, Hawaii, with a diameter of 62mi.

### The highest active volcano
Llullaillaco, Chile, which is 22,058ft high.

### The longest lava flow
The lava flow from the eruption of Laki, Iceland, in 1783, which flowed 43.5mi.

### The largest crater
The largest crater, or caldera, is that of Toba, Indonesia, which covers 1,103mi.

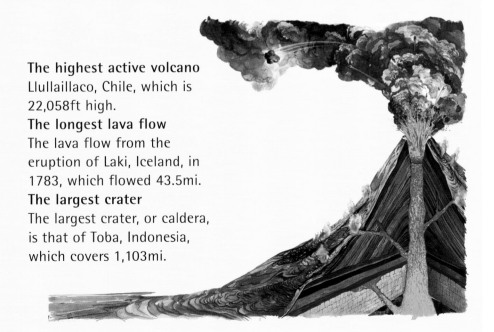

# INDEX

cornea 82-3
corona 126-7
corpus callosum 88
cosmetics 74
costumes 74-5
cotton 20
covalent bond 153
coypu 59
crabs 54-5
crater 104
cretaceans 62
Cretaceous Period 94-5
crevasses 112-3
crinoids 97
crinoline 75
crocodile 48-9
crops 16-7, 70
crusafontia 94
crust (Earth) 100, 102, 105-6
crustaceans 62
Culpeper, Nicholas 19
cuneiform 73
Curie, Marie 155
cyan 83
cyanobacteria 96
cyberspace 167
cycads 10
Cygnus 139

# D

Dalton, John 154
Dark Matter 143
Dartmoor, England 109
date palm 13
daylight 83, 168
deadly nightshade 19
Death Valley, California 31 52
decibels 85, 171

deciduous forests 14
deer 41
delta 111
Deneb 145
denim 75
dentine 77
desert 30-1, 52-3, 114-5
desert hedgehog 53
Devonian Period 95
dicotyledons 11
digestive system 76
digitalis 18, 23
dimetrodon 94
dingo 56
dinosaur 48, 67, 94, 97, 99, 143
distributaries 111
doe 41
dolphin 62-3
Doppler effect 170
downs 28
drupes 13, 23
duck-billed platypus 57
ducks 58

# E

ear 84-5
ear canal 84
eardrum 84
Earth 94-5, 100-1, 122-7, 130-7, 142, 145, 162, 172
earthquakes 100, 106-7
earwax 84
Easter Island 68
eating 76-7
ebb tide 117
echinoderms 62
echo 170
eclipse 125
edelweiss 32-3

Edinburgh Castle 105
Einstein, Albert 174
electricity 164-6, 174
electromagnet 173
electromagnetic spectrum 168-9
electromagnetism 147, 158-9
electronics 166-7
electrons 152-5
element 154-5
elephant 46-7
elk 43
emergent layer (rain forest) 25
emmer 16, 70
Emperor penguins 45
emu 77
enamel 77
Enceladus 137
energy 156-7
engine 160-1
Eon 94
epicenter 106
epiglottis 76
epiphytes 24
Epochs 94
equator 122
erosion 108
eucalyptus 15, 20
evening primrose 31
evergreen 14
exfoliation 109
eye 82-3

# F

Fahrenhiet 156
fallow 17
Faraday, Michael 165
farms 70-1

maize 16
malaria 19
Mammoth Cave, Kentucky 119
mammoths 97
mantle (Earth) 100-1, 106
Maoris 68
maple 14-5
mariner 2,10 131
Mars 122, 128, 131, 134-5
Mars Pathfinder 135
marsupial mole 57
marsupials 56
Masai 68
mass 158
matter 150-1
Matterhorn 51, 109
meander 110-1
melting point 151
menstruation 90
Mercury 122, 128, 134-5
mercury 151, 156
merychippus 94
mesolithic 67
Mesopotamia 71
mesquite 30
mestizos 69
metal 154-5
meteorite 94-5, 134
methane 137
microwaves 129, 133, 168
Milankovitch cycles 113
Milky Way 128, 142-3, 147,
minerals 100
Mir space station 131
mirror 169
mirrors 343
Mississippi River 111
mistletoe 23
mitosis 91
moa 235
Mohenjo-Daro 73

Mohorovicic discontinuity 101
Mojave desert 31
molecules 150, 153
mollusk 55, 62
momentum 159-60
Mongols 68
monocotyledons 11
monotreme 57
month 125
Moon 117, 124-5, 127-8, 130-2, 144-5
moonlight 124
moons 137
moose 43
moraine 112-3
morphine 18
mosses 10-1
mountain goat 51
mountain hare 51
mountains 102-3, 108
mountain plants 32-3
movement 160-1
Mt. Everest 102
Mt. Fujiyama 103-5
Mt. Kenya 33
Mt. Kilimanjaro 46, 104
Mt. McKinlay 103
mucus 86
mudskipper 49
muscle 80-1
mushroom rock 114-5
myofibrils 81
myosin 81

# N

nappe 102
Neanderthal Man 66-7
nebulae 138, 141
Neolithic 67

Neptune 131, 136-7
nerves 89
nervous system 88
neurons 88
neutrinos 153
neutrons 152-4, 175
Nevadian 103
névé 112
New Forest 41
New York 99
Newton, Isaac 158-61
newtons 159
nickel 100
noble gases 154-5
nomads 68
Norfolk, England 113
North Pole 173
northern lights (see Aurora Borealis)
nuclear fission 174-5
nuclear fusion 174
nuclear fusion reaction 138
nuclear power 174-5
nuclear power station 174
nucleus 152, 174-5
nueé ardenté 105

# O

oasis 31, 114-5
Oaxaca 69
observatory 128
oesophagus 76
Ohain, Pabst von 161
Okavango Delta, Botswana 49
olfactory epithelium 86
Olympus Mons 135
Open Universe 147
opium 18
Oppenheimer, Robert 175

reindeer 43
resin 96
resistance 165
resultant 159
retina 82
rib 80
Richter scale 107
Ring of Fire 105
River Nile 111, 114
rivers 110-1
robot 167
rock 96, 102-104, 114-5,
    124, 134
rock arch 116-7
rock pool 54-5
rocket 130, 132-3
Rocky Mountains 102
rods 83
rokerboom 28
ROM 167

# S

S waves 106
Saami 75
saguaro 30-4
Sahara desert 31, 53, 68, 99
    114-5
saliva 76, 86
salmon 59
salt molecules 153
San Andreas fault 99, 107
sand 116
sand cat 52
sand dunes 114-5
sapwood 14
Sarawak Chamber, Malaysia
    119
sari 74
satellite 131-3
Saturn 128, 131-2, 136-7,

sauropods 97
scabious 29
scorpion 53
scree 108
sea lion 45
sea urchin 55
seal 44
seashore 54-5
seasons 123
seaweed 10-1
sediment 102, 111, 157
seeds (plant) 11-3, 16, 23
seifs 115
seismometer 106-7
self-pollination 12
semicircular canals 84-5
semiconductors 166
sense receptors 87
sepal 12
sequoia tree 15
setts 40
shadow 168
shark 62-3
shingle 116
short sight 83
sickle 71
silage 16
silica 104
silicon 140
silicon chip 166
silk 75
silt 110
Silurian Period 95
Sirius, Dog Star 139
skeleton 80
skull 80
sloth 39
smell 86-7
smoking 79
snout (glacier) 112-3
snow leopard 51

snowline 33, 103
snowshoe hare 44
sodium 153
sodium chloride 155
softwood 20
SOHO space telescope 129
solar eclipse 125, 127
solar flares 127
solar prominences 127
solar system 122, 134-5,
    137, 142, 145
solar wind 125, 172
solid 150-1
solute 163
solution 162-3
solvent 163
sonic boom 171
sooty tern 55
sound 84-5, 170-1
sound barrier 171
space labs 131
space probe 134
space shuttle 130-1
space stations 131
spacecraft 130-1, 134, 136
spawn 59
speed of sound 171
sperm 90
spine 80
spoonbill 49
spores 11
spring tide 117
springbok 60-1
springs 110
Sputnik 1 and 2 130, 132,
spy satellites 133
squid 63
stack 116-7
stalactites 118-9
stalagmites 118-9
stamens 12

vixen 41
volcanoes 101, 104-6, 118, 122, 124, 134-5
vomit 77
Voyager space probe 131,137
vulcanologists 105
vultures 52-3

# W

wadi 115
wallaby 57
water 11, 122, 150-1, 155, 162-3
water cycle 150-1
water hyacinth 26
water table 118
water vole 59
waterfall 111, 118
wavelength 168-9
waves 117
waxwing 13
weathering 108-9
weight 158
wetlands 48-9
whale 62-3
wheat 16-3
wheel 71
white dwarfs 138, 141
Whittle, Frank 161
wildebeest 47, 60
willow 18
window plant 31
winds 136
wolves 43
wombat 56
wood mice 41
wood sorrel 23
woodland 22-3, 40-1
woodpecker 40
writing 73

# X

X-ray 129, 169
xylem 11, 15

# Y

yak 50
Yeager, Chuck 171
Yosemite dome, California 109

# Z

zebra 47
ziggurat 73